GW00691912

# GREEN, ROUGH & BUNKER

# GREEN, ROUGH & BUNKER

## A GOLFER'S COMPANION

COMPILED BY
CHRISTINA KONING

MICHAEL O'MARA BOOKS LIMITED

First published in Great Britain in 2000 by
Michael O'Mara Books Limited
9 Lion Yard
Tremadoc Road
London SW4 7NQ

A CIP catalogue record for this book is available from the British Library

ISBN 1-85479-580-5

1 3 5 7 9 10 8 6 4 2

Designed and typeset by Design 23
Printed and bound in Finland by WS Bookwell, Juva

# CONTENTS

# INTRODUCTION

'What earthly good is golf? Life is stern and life is earnest. We live in a practical age. All round us we see foreign competition making itself unpleasant. And we spend our time playing golf! What do we get out of it? Is golf any use? That's what I'm asking you. Can you name me a single case where devotion to this pestilential pastime has done a man any practical good?' . . .

P. G. Wodehouse – from *The Clicking of Cuthbert*

Golf is a game which arouses strong passions. It is nothing but a waste of time, say its detractors; it is impossible; futile; absurd. It spoils what would otherwise be a good walk; it wrecks marriages and undermines friendships. What is the point of golf, these people ask – is it even a proper sport? How can one be serious about a game which involves hitting a very small ball with an oddly shaped stick into an even smaller hole, and in which the aim is to achieve as low a score as possible?

If the things people who don't play golf say about the game are bad enough (and the illustrious golf-haters referred to above include Mark Twain and Winston Churchill), they are nothing to the vitriolic things said about golf by golfers. Golf is 'obsessional, vile, encourages gambling [and] leads to bad language,' opines Michael Green, author of the (admittedly tongue-in-cheek) *The Art of Coarse Golf*. 'On a bad day, golf has a fury that would frighten Lucifer himself,' agrees golf writer Tom O'Connor. Both would doubtless concur with Sir Henry Rider Haggard, whose matchless 'Golf for Duffers' is included here, that golf can ruin your life: 'Drink, opium, gambling – from the clutches of all these it is possible to escape, but from golf, never.'

In making this selection, I have tried to convey something of the love-hate relationship which lies at the heart of so much golfing humour. The self-deprecatory wit with which golfers disparage their successes, and exaggerate their failures, is as much a part of the game as the wearing of tasselled loafers, or the superstitious preference for a favourite cleek. Whether the game is being played on the windswept scrub of the Scottish Lowlands, or the lushly cultivated turf of the Florida Keys, the philosophical turn of mind which golf inspires in its aficionados is the same. There can be few games in which the mood can swing from ridiculous optimism to hopeless cynicism within a matter of seconds, and where pride is almost invariably followed by a fall. The first section of this book reflects these extremities of triumph and despair – as experienced by some of the golfing world's most famous players, as well as some of its anonymous wits.

The mordant humour with which most golfers deal with the highs and lows of the game also features in a lot of golfing fiction. From Robert Marshall's comic novel, *The Haunted Major*, in which a self-satisfied sporting champion discovers that golf may be the one sport he is no good at, to P. G. Wodehouse's hilarious short story, 'A Woman is Only a Woman', in which two friends agree to decide which of them shall get the girl by means of a Trial by Golf, golf has inspired some of the funniest fiction ever written. Gerald Batchelor's depiction of a truly eccentric match in 'One-Ball Golf', Stephen Leacock's tale of golfing obsession, 'The Golfomaniac' and Harry Graham's delightfully quirky 'Retired Golf' – to name but three of those collected here – are classic examples of the comic short story.

Nor is humour the only genre favoured by writers on golf; a whole section of an anthology such as this might as easily be devoted to the 'golfing thriller'. Malcolm Hamer, an extract from whose novel, *Death Trap* – a murder mystery set at the Ryder Cup – is included here, has made a career of writing whodunits with a golfing theme, following the lead of Agatha Christie, whose *Murder on the Links*, featuring her famously laconic Belgian sleuth Hercule Poirot, was first published in 1923. Other writers – notably Ian Fleming in *Goldfinger* (also represented here) – have chosen to set entire chapters of their novels on the links, rightly judging that nothing would convey the drama of a conflict between two deadly adversaries better than a golf match.

Indeed, one might conceivably regard the stories in this anthology as belonging to a literary tradition – the knightly quest – as old as the game of golf itself. For there is certainly an heroic (or at least mock-heroic) quality about all of them, describing, as they do, a game that involves both luck and skill, in which two or more protagonists set out across a perilous landscape, in search of a seemingly unattainable prize. The tale of Sir Lancelot and Sir Galahad, or of Don Quixote and Sancho Panza – what else are these but golfing stories, with swords and lances taking the place of putters and mashie niblicks, and the perils of enchanted forests and bottomless lakes standing in for those of the sand-trap and the dog-leg hole?

CHRISTINA KONING
*June 2000*

# Sayings, Anecdotes, Jokes and Verse

'Golf is a good walk spoiled.'
MARK TWAIN

'Golf is a game whose aim is to hit a very small ball into an even smaller hole with weapons singularly ill-designed for the purpose.'
WINSTON CHURCHILL

'Club – kind of stick used in golf.'
OXFORD ENGLISH DICTIONARY

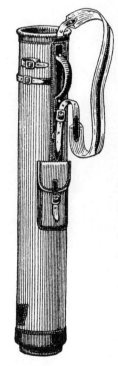

'The ball no question makes of Ayes and Noes,
But Here or There strikes as the player goes.'
– FROM THE RUBÁIYÁT OF OMAR KHAYYÁM,
TRANSLATED BY EDWARD FITZGERALD

'It's often necessary to hit a second drive to really appreciate the first one.'
ANON.

'I've seen lifelong friends drift apart over golf just because one could play better, but the other counted better.'
STEPHEN LEACOCK

'To the immortal memory of JOHN HENRIE and PAT ROGIE who at Edinburgh in the year AD 1593 were imprisoned for "Playing of the gowff on the links of Leith every Sabbath the time of the sermonses", also of ROBERT ROBERTSON who got it in the neck in AD 1604 for the same reason.'
P.G. WODEHOUSE – DEDICATION TO THE CLICKING OF CUTHBERT

'I get upset over a bad shot just like anyone else. But it's silly to let the game get to you. When I miss a shot I just think what a beautiful day it is. And what pure fresh air I'm breathing. Then I take a deep breath. I have to do that. That's what gives me the strength to break the club.'
BOB HOPE – FROM CONFESSIONS OF A HOOKER

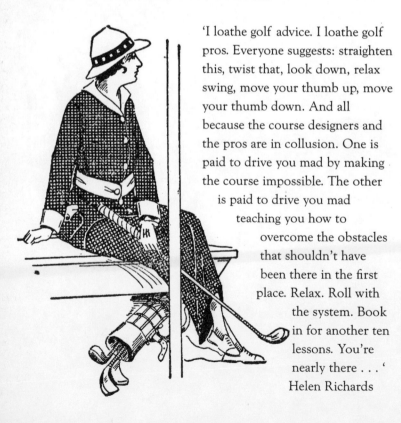

'I loathe golf advice. I loathe golf pros. Everyone suggests: straighten this, twist that, look down, relax swing, move your thumb up, move your thumb down. And all because the course designers and the pros are in collusion. One is paid to drive you mad by making the course impossible. The other is paid to drive you mad teaching you how to overcome the obstacles that shouldn't have been there in the first place. Relax. Roll with the system. Book in for another ten lessons. You're nearly there . . . '
Helen Richards

'Gene Littler swings a golf club with the same elegant style as Sinatra brings to a song, Nureyev to a dance, Olivier to a Shakespearian role. If his swing were a piece of music, it would be a Strauss waltz.'
NICK SEITZ

'Golf – can we please address the myth that this is a sport? These people are dressed in street clothes. They are never out of breath. Some of them are wearing saddle shoes. They have servants to carry their equipment.'
MIKE ROYKO

'A golf course is the epitome of all that is purely transitory in the universe, a space not to dwell in, but to get over as soon as possible.'
JEAN GIRAUDOUX

'The newly converted golf enthusiast was introducing his wife to the game. He had expounded at great length on what a fine exercise golf was, the beauty of the countryside and the joy of being "out in the open". On the first tee he prepared to give his first demonstration of the game itself. Taking his stance he swung hard – and missed. Embarrassed, he reorganized his stance and swung again. Again he missed. His third effort was also a wiff. At this point his bride asked innocently, "George, I can see that golf is a fine exercise. *But what's the little ball for?*"'
SEYMOUR DUNN – FROM *THE COMPLETE GOLF JOKE BOOK*

'Golf – a game played by placing a small ball, one and a half inches in diameter, on top of a big ball, 8,000 miles in diameter, and trying to knock the small ball off the big ball rather than vice versa.'
FRED BECK AND O.K. BARNES – FROM *SEVENTY-FIVE YEARS IN A SAND TRAP*

'It took me 17 years to get 3,000 hits in baseball. I did it in one afternoon on the golf course.'
HENRY AARON (BASEBALL'S ALL-TIME HOME-RUN LEADER)

'You drive for show and putt for dough.'
SAM SNEAD

'Golf is the hardest game in the world. There is no way you can ever get it. Just when you think you do, the game jumps up and puts you in your place.'
BEN CRENSHAW

'If you're going to throw a club, it is important to throw it ahead of you, down the fairway, so you don't have to waste energy going back to pick it up.'
TOMMY BOLT

'Victory is everything. You can spend the money, but you can never spend the memories.'
KEN VENTURI

'Putts get real difficult the day they hand out the money.'
LEE TREVINO

'If all the golfers in the world could be laid end to end, I for one would leave them there.'
MICHAEL PARKINSON

'Golf is obsessional, vile, encourages gambling on the course and in the clubhouse, leads to bad language, the expenditure of a great deal of money (most of it wasted) and has wrecked many marriages. I cannot understand why anyone plays it. In fact the only reason I am spending my holidays golfing this year is because I'm convinced that with a bit of practice I can cure my hook. I'm

sure I'm standing too close to the ball and relaxing the knees too much. I think that if I took up a more open stance and moved the front foot . . . '
MICHAEL GREEN – FROM *THE ART OF COARSE GOLF*

'A game of golf is usually played between two, sometimes four friends. Each player tries to urge his golf ball into a special hole in the grass by tapping it with one of his bundle of sticks. When the ball eventually drops into the hole the golfer remembers the number of whacks it took him and if his friend is watching, writes that number down on his scorecard. After doing this eighteen times the friends add up their scores to find the winner. As in receiving a prison sentence, or the news of a multiple birth of offspring, a low number is hoped for. After working out who is the winner, the losers all say "Well done!" and silently accompany their ex-friend back to the clubhouse.'
FRANK MUIR – FROM *ONE OVER PAR*

'A guy works till he has the ball going where he wants every time, and then he says "I'm gonna stretch it out a little longer," and he's lost it.'
GARDNER DICKINSON

'A golfer, who had a powerful telescope, invited his caddie to take a look at the moon. "Faith, sir," said the caddie. "She's terrible fu' o' bunkers!"'
ANON.

'Golf is like a love affair: if you don't take it seriously, it's no fun; if you do take it seriously it breaks your heart.'
ARNOLD DALY

'Do not be tempted to invest in a sample of each golfing invention as soon as it makes its appearance. If you do, you will only complicate and spoil your game – and encumber your locker with much useless rubbish.'
HARRY VARDON

'Golf is not, on the whole, a game for realists. By its exactitudes of measurement, it invites the attention of perfectionists.'
HEYWOOD HALE BROWN

'The game of golf is 90 per cent mental and 10 per cent mental.'
THOMAS MULLIGAN

'The least thing upsets him on the links. He misses short putts because of the uproar of the butterflies in the surrounding meadows.'
P.G. WODEHOUSE – FROM THE CLICKING OF CUTHBERT

'Bob Hope tells the story that his doctor told him he was overworked for a man in his eighties and needed a complete rest – and that included giving up golf. Hope decided to give up his doctor instead. He tried a second opinion and a third, and on the fourth try he found a doctor who told him he could play eighteen holes whenever he felt like it. Hope says he actually hugged the man and said "Thanks doc, just for that I'll remember you in my will." And the doctor said, "In that case, play thirty-six."'
BOB MONKHOUSE

'In 1912 an American enthusiast made golfing history, when she took 166 strokes over a 130-yard hole. During the qualifying round of the Shawnee Invitational for Ladies at Shawnee-on-Delaware, Pennsylvania, she confidently approached the sixteenth hole for which four strokes were normally adequate. Her first shot, however, sent the ball into the Binniekill River, an obstacle which many would regard as final.

When she saw that it floated she boarded a rowing boat, with her husband at the oars and herself at the prow, wielding a golf club. For one and a half miles her husband rowed and kept count of the occasions on which she had occasion to swipe at it.

Eventually, she beached the thing and made her way back through a forest. Fellow competitors had given up hope of ever seeing her again, when they heard the cry of 'fore' and saw the ball fly on the green from a totally unexpected direction. She completed the hole in just under two hours.'

STEPHEN PILE – FROM *THE BOOK OF HEROIC FAILURES*

'In 1976 Mr Maurice Flitcroft, a 46-year-old crane driver from Barrow-in-Furness, made history by taking a record 121 strokes in the first qualifying round at Formby in Lancashire. So upset were the championship committee when they heard this that they refunded the £30 entry fees to the two golfers drawn to play with him. "I enjoyed the game," said Mr Flitcroft afterwards. "It was good practice."'

– ABRIDGED FROM THE ABOVE

'The City Golf Club in London is unique among such organizations in not possessing a golf course, ball, tee, caddie or bag. Its whole premises just off Fleet Street do not contain a single photograph of anything that approaches a golfing topic.

"We had a driving range once," the commissionaire said, "but we dropped that years ago." The membership now devotes itself exclusively to eating and drinking.'

IBID.

'Golf is an exercise which is much used by the Gentlemen in Scotland. A large common, in which there are several little holes, is chosen for the purpose. It is played with little leather balls stuffed with feathers, and sticks tipped with horn. He who putts with the fewest strokes gets the game . . . A man would live ten years longer for using this exercise once or twice a week.'
DR BENJAMIN BUSH – FROM *SERMONS TO GENTLEMEN ABOUT TEMPERANCE AND EXERCISE* (1772)

'Putting is like wisdom, partly a natural gift and partly the accumulation of experience.'
ARNOLD PALMER

'At Jinga there is both hotel and golf course. The latter is, I believe, the only course in the world which posts a special rule that the player may remove his ball from hippopotamus footprints.'
EVELYN WAUGH

'It might have been Arnie Palmer or then again it could have been Gary Player – anyhow it was one of the famous professionals . . .

He hit his drive deep into the woods for the third time that day.

"The number four axe, I think," he said with aplomb, turning to his caddie.'
– FROM *WORLD'S BEST GOLF JOKES*

'"What a mess I'm making of it," said a disgruntled golfer to his caddie. "Do you think anybody could play worse than I've been doing?" The caddie had been accustomed to speak the plain truth. "Oh, weel, there may be worse players," he answered, "but it's likely they dinna try to play."'
FROM *TOLD AT THE NINETEENTH: HUMOROUS ST ANDREWS STORIES*

'Sherriff— was on the bench when young Robbie Black was called as a witness. "Do you understand the nature of an oath?" gravely asked his Honour. "Oh ay, sir," answered Robbie with equal gravity, "I've carried your clubs mony a time."'
IBID.

'He plays a fair game of golf – if you watch him.'
ANON.

'Last week I missed a spectacular hole in one – by only five strokes.'
ANON.

'My golf is definitely improving. I'm missing the ball much closer than I used to.'
ANON.

'You can always tell a golfer who's winning. He's the one who keeps telling his opponent that it's only a game.'
ANON.

'As they left the church on the way to the reception, the groom turned to the bride and said, "I've got a confession to make: I love golf. I sleep, eat, and breathe golf. I'm obsessed with golf. You must realize that it completely dominates my life."

And the bride turned to the groom and said, "Thank you for being so honest. Now I have something to tell you: I'm a hooker."

"No problem," the groom said, taking her wrists. "You hold your left hand just a little higher than the right, with your thumb down here . . . "'

ANON.

'A keen golfer goes to a priest and asks him if there are any golf courses in Heaven. The priest says he'll find out for him. The next day, the priest calls the golfer and says, "I've done some checking up and I've got some good news and some bad news. The good news is that there are golf courses in Heaven and they're far better than any golf course we have down here."

The golfer says, "So what's the bad news?"

And the priest says, "The bad news is that you've got a teeing-off time for next Monday afternoon."'

– FROM *REALLY WICKED GOLF JOKES*

Golfer: 'I've never played this badly before.'
Caddie: 'You've played before?'
IBID.

Golfer: 'That can't be my ball, caddie. It looks far too old.'
Caddie: 'It's a long time since we started, sir.'
IBID.

Golfer: 'What a disastrous round. You must be the worst caddie in the world!'
Caddie: 'I doubt it, sir. That would be too much of a coincidence!'
IBID.

'Nothing counts in a golf game like your opponent.'
IBID.

'Golf is a lot of walking, broken up by disappointment and bad arithmetic.'
IBID.

'Definition of a golf ball: a small object that remains on the tee while a perspiring citizen fans it vigorously with a large club.'
IBID.

First man: 'My doctor has told me that I can't play golf.'
Second man: 'So he's played with you too, has he?'
IBID.

First man: 'It's hard to believe that old Harry is dead. And to think he was going to play golf with us tomorrow. It's awful!'
Second man: 'Yes, it's tragic! But wait a minute . . . Maybe we can get Mike to fill in for him.'
IBID.

'When her husband arrived home from the golf course several hours late, his wife demanded an explanation.
   "We had a problem," he said. "Frank collapsed and died on the second hole and from then on it was play the ball, drag Frank, play the ball, drag Frank . . . "'
IBID.

'I was playing golf with a friend the other day and, just as we were about to tee off, a funeral procession went by.

My friend put his club down, took off his cap and bowed his head as the cortège passed us.

I said, "That was a very decent gesture."

And he said, "It was the least I could do. She was a damned good wife to me."'

IBID.

'An English professor who was teaching at an American university was invited by a member of the college golf team to come out and play golf for the first time. They arrived at the course and the professor asked the student, "What do I do?"

"You have to hit the ball towards the flag over there on the green," the student explained.

So the professor carefully teed up his ball and proceeded to drive it straight down the fairway. The ball rolled on to the green where it came to a stop less than an inch from the hole.

"Well, what do I do now?" he asked the amazed student.

"You're supposed to hit the ball into the cup," he said.

"Oh, great!" exclaimed the professor. "Now you tell me!"'

IBID.

'Robinson Crusoe-style, the shipwrecked golfer made the best of his tiny island. When a cruise liner spotted his distress signals and sent a boat to investigate, the landing party was amazed to find a crude but recognizable nine-hole course which the castaway had played with driftwood woods, whalebone and coral putter and balls carved out of pumice stone.

"Quite a layout," said the officer in charge of the rescuers.

"Too kind, it's very rough and ready," the goatskin-clad golfer responded. Then he smiled slyly. "But I am quite proud of the water hazard . . . "'

– FROM A ROUND OF GOLF JOKES

'To kick off their wedding reception, bride Christyne Curley Velez, a 31-handicapper, challenged her new husband, Bill Velez, a 26-handicapper, to a one-hole match on the par-5, 515-yard eighteenth hole at Sterling Farms Golf Club.

The wedding guests cheered the newlyweds as they headed for the tee. Still wearing her floor-length chiffon wedding gown and wielding her Big Bertha, Christyne banged her tee shot 175 yards down the right side of the fairway. Velez, wearing tux and tails, outgunned her by 25 yards with a 200-yard drive.

Christyne eventually reached the back fringe of the green in four shots, then nearly got her par when her chip shot struck the flag and bounced a few inches from the hole. She made a bogey six – and put the pressure squarely on the groom, who was languishing in a greenside bunker in three shots.

Bill, though, managed to extricate himself with a blast that put the ball on to the green in four, 30 feet from the hole. Now came the big question: would he nail the long putt and upstage his wife only minutes after exchanging their wedding vows? Or would he do the gentlemanly thing and three-putt, making the new missus happy in his first official act as a husband?

Bill did neither. Instead, he knocked his first putt 29 feet and then made the 1-foot tap-in for a bogey.

The newlyweds had tied not only the knot but the match.'
– FROM THE GOLF NUT'S BOOK OF AMAZING FEATS

'Well-known Scottish golfer David Struth bet friends that he could play St Andrews in less than 100 strokes – at night under a full moon.

He beat his goal by seven shots. And amazingly, he shot his 93 without losing the ball.'
IBID.

'It was the first golfing day of the new season and Pete couldn't wait to get out on the course. He had spent the whole winter practising indoors, working on his swing and his putting. He had even invested a small fortune to go to one of those fancy golf schools for an intensive two weeks of one-on-one tuition, and he was ready.

He headed out with his caddie and, around about the sixth hole, he turned to the caddie, who up until then, hadn't had much to say, and puffing his chest up with pride, said to him, "So, tell me, have you noticed anything different since last year?"

"Yes, sir, I certainly have," said the caddie.

"And what's that?" Pete asked smugly.

"You've had your clubs regripped."'

– FROM *REALLY WICKED GOLF JOKES*

'At first a golfer excuses a dismal performance by claiming bad lies. With experience, he covers up with better ones.'

P. BROWN

'The difference between learning to drive a car and learning to play golf is that in golf you never hit anything.'

– FROM *A ROUND OF GOLF JOKES*

'If you watch a game, it's fun. If you play it, it's recreation. If you work at it, it's golf.'

BOB HOPE

'It's good sportsmanship not to pick up lost golf balls while they are still rolling.'

MARK TWAIN

'Back at the nineteenth, in a vile mood, he delivered his bitter tale of woe.

"Nothing could stop me winning. I had a putt of about eleven inches, hardly more than a tap-in, to clinch it. The green was dead flat, perfectly true, a real billiard table. Not a breath of wind.

"My ball was heading for the cup, on rails. Then a raven swooped down snatched it up, and circled the flag stick, twice. The raven passed the ball to a vulture, which flapped over to Paradise Brook, opened its talons and . . . splash. End of story."

St Peter sighed deeply and vowed, "Last time I ever play St Francis of Assisi."'
– FROM *A ROUND OF GOLF JOKES*

'I don't say that my golf game is bad, but if I grew tomatoes, they'd come up sliced.'
MILLER BARBER

'The truly great things happen when a genius is alone. This is true especially among golfers.'
J.R. COULSON

'Golf appeals to the idiot in us, and the child. What child does not grasp the pleasure-principle of miniature golf? Just how childlike golf players become is proven by their frequent inability to count past five.'
JOHN UPDIKE

'We all have stupid genes in us, and golf brings out those stupid genes.'
JOHN MADDEN

'When miracles happen on the golf course, it is important to know how to respond to them.

Songwriter Hoagy Carmichael, an avid golfer, once teed up on a par-three hole, picked up a club and hit the ball. It bounced once on the green, hit the pin and dropped in for a hole in one. Hoagy didn't say a word, but took another ball from his pocket, teed up, then observed, "I think I've got the idea now."'

BUDDY HACKET – FROM THE TRUTH ABOUT GOLF AND OTHER LIES

'Penalties must be provided to exact a toll for those who make mistakes, yet not so severe nor of a nature that will prohibit a full recovery by the execution of an unusually well-played shot.'

DONALD ROSS

'In 1986-7, when the Cunard liner QE2 was being refitted, sets of golf clubs were made from the bronze alloy of her original propellers by Swilken, clubmakers of St Andrews. Each set, which was badged with the QE2's logo, consisted of fourteen clubs and was priced at a whacking US$16,500, although to be fair Swilken did throw in a bag, umbrella, a dozen balls and other goodies – all bearing the Cunarder's symbol, of course.'

– FROM THE GOLF NUT'S BOOK OF AMAZING FEATS AND RECORDS

'Although recognized as one of the world's greatest dancers, Fred Astaire was also a fine golfer – and he proved his prowess with both his club and his feet in a remarkable dance sequence in the 1938 film Carefree.

The script called for Astaire, at a golf club, to dance atop tables and furniture, glide down halls, bound out onto the terrace, and tap his way to the practice range where he was to hit a dozen golf balls while still dancing.

To make the golfing portion of the dance routine – which was shot on a course in Pasadena – more compelling, Astaire and director Mark Sandrich decided to shoot it in one continuous scene. There would be no stopping and no cuts.

The camera started rolling. With music blaring from an outdoor loudspeaker to help him keep a beat, Astaire grabbed a driver and tap-danced his way up to a line of twelve teed-up balls. Moving to the music, Astaire deftly and rhythmically kept dancing while whacking the balls in succession towards a practice green. He didn't miss a beat – or a ball. It was a perfect take.

When some members of the crew went to retrieve the balls, they were astounded at what they saw. All dozen balls were lying on the green – within eight feet of each other!'

IBID.

'Golf is the best of games, golf is the worst of games.

On a bad day, golf has a fury that would frighten Lucifer himself.

On a good day, golf has a serenity seemingly bestowed by the angels.

It has heights of ecstasy and lows of despair, and extreme swings of temperament such as are unknown to any other sport.

Golf is the last bastion of sportsmanship, fair play and competitiveness.

Golf is also wide open to abuse, score manipulation and law-breaking.

It has a language and a humour all its own – "He's the type of golfer who shouts 'Fore!' shoots six and puts down five on his card . . ."'

TOM O'CONNOR – FROM *FROM THE WOOD TO THE TEES*

'At least he can't cheat on his score – because all you have to do is look down the fairway and count the wounded.'

BOB HOPE, ON THE THEN US VICE-PRESIDENT, SPIRO T. AGNEW

'What we've got in [Craig] Stadler is a guy who looks like everybody's tough bartender with a sunburned neck and the forearms of a jackhammer jockey.'

THOMAS BOSWELL

'Bobby Jones and Harry Vardon combined exquisiteness of art with utterly relentless precision in a way not given to other golfers.'
BERNARD DARWIN

'[Seve] Ballesteros's game seems to come from inside him. He seems to produce shots by subconscious force, by will.'
MICHAEL BAMBURGER – FROM *TO THE LINKSLAND*

'Satan, fuming, called a staff meeting. Hades had become too soft an option, he scolded, due to their fiendish complacency and idleness. Every little devil must tighten up, crack down, and give guests a hell of a time, he decreed. "I want them tested to the limit, tormented, humiliated – but the twist is, you must hold out a false promise that things will get better."

"Like in golf, eh?" a fork-tailed junior executive suggested, anxious to show he had caught on.

And Satan, taken aback, spluttered, "Hold on, nothing *that* strong, old son. They're only human and they have to last out for eternity, remember . . . "'
– FROM *A ROUND OF GOLF JOKES*

'Give me golf clubs, fresh air and a beautiful partner, and you can keep the golf clubs and the fresh air.'
JACK BENNY

'"If I died, would you remarry?" asked the wife.

"Probably would," came the reply.

"And would you let her be your golfing partner?"

"Yes, I think so."

"But surely you wouldn't give her my clubs?"

"Oh no. She's left-handed."'
– FROM *WORLD'S BEST GOLF JOKES*

'Niggled by impatience and open hostility in the lengthening line behind him, Wally Wimpe lowered his club, looked back and said haughtily, "I'm entitled to take my time over addressing the ball."

"Quick, somebody remind him where the ball lives," came a weary appeal from the back of the crowd.'
– FROM A ROUND OF GOLF JOKES

'A wife always knows when her husband has had a bad round. He has pond weed in his socks.'
P. BROWN

'"How are you getting on with your new clubs?" asked the golfer when he walked into the bar and saw a friend of his. "Fine," replied the friend. "They put twenty yards on my slice."'
DAI REES – FROM DAI REES ON GOLF

'Golf is a non-violent game played violently from within.'
BOB TOSKI

'Phil and Tony had arranged a game of golf at the club. When they met at the first tee, Phil was surprised to see Tony standing there with not one but two caddies at his side. They teed off and were about half-way round the course when Phil could not contain his curiosity any longer.

"What's this, then?" asked Phil. "Did you win the lottery or something?"

"What do you mean?" asked Tony.

"You know what I mean," said Phil. "The two caddies. Why are you using two caddies?"

"Oh, them," said Tony. "My wife was complaining I wasn't spending enough time with the kids."'
– FROM REALLY WICKED GOLF JOKES

'The hacker came upon a hole that was famously said to possess the world's largest fairway bunker. Naturally, his tee shot, as if drawn by a magnet, found its way right into the heart of this monster. As they reached the abyss, the hacker peered over the edge and turned to his caddie.

"What club do you suggest?" he asked.

"Well, sir, it doesn't really matter much," the caddie replied, "but may I suggest that you don't go in there without an adequate supply of food and water?"'

IBID.

'There once was a caddie with a reputation for using strong language on the course. He was assigned to caddie for the local Anglican bishop, and warned by the caddiemaster to say nothing unless spoken to, and above all not to swear.

Things went well for a couple of holes. Then on the third the bishop's stroke was not quite clean.

"Where did that sod go, caddie?" asked the churchman, looking to replace a divot he'd shifted.

"Into the bloody bunker," retorted the caddie who'd watched the ball. "And don't forget you started it."'

– FROM WORLD'S BEST GOLF JOKES

'The Rev. Robert MacPherson was an earnest and conscientious minister, who learned, during a visit to St Andrews, to play golf after a fashion. He was always keenly absorbed in the match and suffered great vexation when he played badly. On one particular day he happened to be in bad form, and committed many golfing faults, getting more and more annoyed with each foozle, but bottling up his feelings with a manifest effort. At last he said desperately to his partner: "This will never do. I'll have to give it up!" "What, give up golf?" asked his partner. "No," said Mr MacPherson dismally, "Give up the ministry."'

IBID.

DUE PRECAUTION TAKEN

'As we drew near the second hole, behold there might be seen,
A lady, with her back to us, *sitting upon the green!*
We shouted "Fore!" with vigour, and more than once indeed;
But, lost in thought, she heard us not, nor took the slightest heed.
She baulked a bold approach for me; but manners still intact,
I thought a word of caution seemed to be the courteous act.
I said, "Excuse me, have you realized the risk you run
By sitting on that green? It is a thing that's seldom done."
She beamed upon me brightly – "Oh, many thanks!" she said,
"But there isn't really any risk – I'm sitting on a plaid."'
– FROM *TOLD AT THE NINETEENTH*

'Old Willie B—, genial soul, liked to encourage the players who
employed him as a caddie, by appreciative comments on the strokes
they played. One day his "man", expending on a tee stroke more
energy and zeal than skilful guidance, carried out a vigorous swing
which was just too high to encounter the ball. "That wad hae been a
splendid shot," chirruped Willie, "if ye had but hit the ba'!"'
IBID.

SHAKESPEARE ON GOLF

All the world knows that Shakespeare was its one universal genius; but probably few have as yet realized the extraordinary range of his knowledge, or the extent of his acquaintance with detail. From his familiarity with every practical pursuit, he is by some supposed to have been a lawyer, by others a doctor, again a sailor, a schoolmaster, a soldier, a printer, an apothecary, a gypsy, a spiritualist. These, however, are but trivial guesses; and it is not only in secondary matters – such as History, Philosophy, Science or Politics supply – that his marvellous knowledge is seen, but also in the far more important sphere of human interest, which relates to the sports and relaxations of the race.

Probably no one – not Gervinus or Schmidt, Cowden-Clarke or even the Bishop of St Andrews – has ever yet surmised that Shakespeare was a Golfer! Proof, however, is abundant that he was not only a distinguished Player, acquainted with all the hazards of the game, but that he knew every peculiarity of the St Andrews Links – that he had experience of all the bunkers, that he was familiar with 'Walkinshaw' and 'the Elysian Fields', that he sometimes drove into the Burn, that he once did the Long Hole in three, and that his lowest score was eighty-two.

It is more than probable that when he visited Scotland as a strolling player and went to Glamis, Dunsinane and Forres, collecting material for *Macbeth*, he also spent some time in the ancient Scottish capital, and solaced himself, after his labours as a playwright and an actor, by an occasional round of the Links.

His familiarity with the old City by the Sea, his allusions to the Castle, with its 'coigns of vantage' and its 'temple-haunting martlets' –
> *This castle hath a pleasant seat,*
etc., etc., are well known to every reader of the Plays. References no less apposite to St Rule, St Salvator and St Leonards, to the Cathedral, the Priory, and the Colleges, are scattered throughout the tragedies and comedies. It will therefore surprise no one to be told that upwards of one hundred allusions to *the noble game* are to be found in Shakespeare, and that he prized Golf more than Archery, or Tennis, or Falconry, or Hunting.

It is unquestionable that the Game of Golf is a mirror of chief incidents and accidents of life; that from the opening tee-shot to the final putt it is a picture of human experience: and, while it may be disputed whether to be a good golfer is necessarily to be a good fellow, every golfing community knows that *the play reveals the man* in a very remarkable manner. Hence it was inevitable that as soon as Shakespeare crossed the Border he should take to the game, and love it, both for its own sake, and for what it reveals of human nature.

What follows is a mere selection of our Dramatist's allusions to
the Green, with its incidents and adventures:

ON THE GAME IN GENERAL:
'Certain issues strokes must arbitrate.'
*Macbeth*, V. iv.

TWO PLAYERS MEETING BY ACCIDENT:
(First) 'Then, shall we have a match?'
*All's Well That Ends Well*, V. iii.
(Second) 'I'll make sport with thee.'
*All's Well That Ends Well*, V. iii.

A REMARKABLY LONG DRIVE FROM THE TEE:
'A hit: a very palpable hit.'
*Hamlet*, V. ii.

PUTTING TOO KEENLY ON A SMOOTH GREEN:
1) 'We may outrun
By violent swiftness that which we run at,
And lose by over-running.'
*Henry VIII*, I. i.
2) 'Too swift arrives as tardy as too slow.'
*Romeo and Juliet*, II. vi

WINNING ONE HOLE BY A STEAL, AND LOSING THE NEXT TWO:
'Did'st thou never hear
That things ill got had ever bad success?'
III *Henry VI*, II. ii.

PRESSING:
'Striving to better, oft we mar what's well.'
*King Lear*, I. iv.

AFTER MISSING A SHORT PUTT, AND STILL THINKING ABOUT IT,
ONE MISSES THE NEXT TEE-STROKE:
'To mourn a mischief that is past and gone
Is the next way to draw new mischief on.'
*Othello*, I. iii.

TAKING THE EYE OFF THE BALL:
'Oft the eye deceives, the mind being troubled.'
*Poems*

LOFTING OVER ONE HAZARD, AND GOING INTO ANOTHER:
'Vaulting ambition . . . o'erleaps itself,
And falls on the other side.'
*Macbeth*, I. vii.

YOU HAVE THE HONOUR:
'Will you shog off?'
*Henry V*, II. i.

A CADDIE IN THE WAY:
'Stand aside, good bearer.'
*Love's Labour's Lost*, IV. i.

WILD DRIVING ON A GUSTY
DAY:
'Still, still, far wide.'
*King Lear*, IV. vii

A LOW-FLYING BALL HIT
STRAIGHT AGAINST THE
WIND:
'He knows the game: how
true he keeps the wind!'
III *Henry VI*, III. ii.

PLAYING FROM THE TEE OPPOSITE
WALKINSHAW, AND GOING INTO
THE BUNKER:
'How oft the sight of means ill
deeds to do
Makes ill deeds done!'
*King John*, IV. ii

IN A BAD BUNKER:
Hamlet: 'Whose grave's this?'
Clown: 'Mine, sir.'
Hamlet: 'I think it be thine,
indeed, for thou liest in't.'
*Hamlet*, V. i.

PLAYING OUT OF A BUNKER IN DRY
WEATHER, AND SENDING THE BALL
DEEPER INTO THE SAND:
'Out of the smoke, into the smother!'
*As You Like It*, I. ii

SEEING A BALL PLAYED TO THE VERY EDGE OF A BUNKER:
'To the extreme edge of hazard.'
*All's Well That Ends Well*, III. iii.

TO A PLAYER WHO ESCAPES MANY HAZARDS:
'Was there ever man had such luck.'
*Cymbeline*, II. i.

AFTER TAKING A GOOD SHOT OUT OF A BUNKER, INTO WHICH A
WEAK SHOT OF YOUR PARTNER SENT YOU:
'I am clear from *his* misdeed.'
*III Henry VI*, III. iii.

WHEN A PLAYER HAS MADE AN UNEXPECTEDLY GOOD STROKE:
'O it is excellent
To have a giant's strength.'
*Measure for Measure*, II. ii

IN A BAD PLACE (TO THE CADDIE):
'Give me the iron, I say.'
*King John*, IV. i.

TO A PLAYER WHO USES HIS IRON IN GRASS,
WHEN HE MIGHT HAVE USED WOOD:
'You spare your spoons.'
*Henry VIII*, V. ii.
(THE REPLY:)
'I have not much skill in grass.'
*All's Well That Ends Well*, IV. v.

ON A ROUGH PUTTING GREEN:
'Uneven is the course, I like it not.'
*Romeo and Juliet*, IV. i.

ON A LEVEL PUTTING GREEN:
'Methinks the ground is even.'
*King Lear*, IV. vi.

LOSING A STROKE, THROUGH WANT OF CONFIDENCE:
'Our doubts are traitors,
And make us lose the good we oft might win
By fearing to attempt.'
*Measure for Measure*, I. v.

A DEAD STYMIE: THE PLAYER TRYING TO LOFT OVER HIS OPPONENT'S BALL:
'Our fortune lies upon this jump.'
*Antony and Cleopatra*, III. viii.

LOSING HOLE AFTER HOLE CONTINUOUSLY:
1) 'One woe doth tread upon another's heel,
So fast they follow.'
*Hamlet*, IV. vii.
2) 'When sorrows come, they come not single spies,
But in battalions.'
*Hamlet*, IV. v.


TAKING THE LAST HOLE IN THREE:
'The daintiest last, to make the end most sweet.'
*Richard II*. I. iii.


AT THE CLOSE OF A MATCH, WHEN YOUR OPPONENT HAS PLAYED WELL,
AND BEATEN YOU:
'The game was ne'er so fair, and I am done.'
*Romeo and Juliet*, I. iv.

THE WINNER, AFTER A STIFF MATCH:
'The harder matched, the greater
victory.'
III *Henry VI*, V. ii.


THE LOSER:
'What foul play had we!'
*The Tempest*, I. ii.


TO THE PLAYER WHO LOSES HIS TEMPER:
'A poor player, that struts and frets.'
*Macbeth*, V. v.


WINNING THE MATCH AT THE LAST HOLE:
'The end crowns all.'
*Troilus and Cressida*, IV. v.

THE DEFEATED PLAYER:
'Things without all remedy
Should be without regard.'
*Coriolanus*, IV. i.

IN THE KITCHEN BEYOND HELL BUNKER:
'He must have a long spoon that must
eat with the Devil.'
*A Comedy of Errors*, IV. iii.

TAKING THE SHORT HOLE IN ONE:
AN IRON SHOT:
'How poor an instrument
May do a noble deed!'
*Antony and Cleopatra*, V. ii.

TO OPPONENT, LOSING TEMPER AT HIS PARTNER'S BAD PLAY, AND
USING STRONG LANGUAGE:
'Good words are better than bad strokes, Octavius.'
*Julius Caesar*, V. i.

THE PLAYER, SEEING HIS BALL DEEPLY BURIED IN A BAD BUNKER:
'Here, in the sands,
Thee I'll rake up.'
*King Lear*, IV. vi.

A PLAYER TO HIS CADDIE, WHO HAS GIVEN HIM A PUTTER, WHEN THE
IRON WAS THE MORE SUITABLE CLUB:
'Sense is not good to give putter.'
*The Merry Wives of Windsor*, V. v.

REMARK IN THE CLUB, AFTER A MATCH, TO AN INDIFFERENT PLAYER:
'You are abused, and by some putter.'
*The Winter's Tale*, II. i.

To opponent, who has taken three holes running by long
flukey putts:
'Thou puttest up thy fortune.'
*Romeo and Juliet*, II. iii.

To one who insists on putting out a hole though playing five
more:
'Now we find
A putter out of five for one.'
*The Tempest*, III. iii.

– from Andrew Lang (ed.), *On The Links – Being Golfing
Stories by Various Hands; with Shakespeare on Golf by A
Novice* (1899)

'In March 1457, King James II of Scotland, learning that his subjects
were devoting too much time to golf at the expense of archery – and
thus of national defence against their constant enemy, England –
issued a decree "that golfe be utterlie cryed down and not used".
James's great-great granddaughter, Mary, Queen of Scots, frequently
ignored affairs of state in favour of time spent on the links, ordering
the sons of French nobles serving at her Court to act as her caddies.
In 1567, only days after the murder of her second husband, Lord
Darnley, she interrupted her mourning in order to get in a few
rounds, to the scandal of many. When she was put on trial in
England for treason, the fact that she had played golf after Darnley's
death was offered as evidence of her cold-heartedness. Executed in
1587 at the instigation of her cousin, Elizabeth I of England, it can
therefore be said that in part she lost her head to golf.'

CRUSHED BY CRUNCH

'A pupil named Townsend from California told me this story one summer while I was teaching at Cherry Hills. Townsend was playing in an amateur match-play tournament at North Berwick in Scotland. He hired a local caddie who was known as Crunch.

Townsend and Crunch set out on a practice round the day before the tournament. It was Townsend's first visit to North Berwick, and he was awed by treading the ground that had been walked on by so many of the giants of the game since the invention of golf. I have heard Ben Crenshaw say he thinks North Berwick is one of the best courses in the world.

Townsend said his feeling of reverence crept into his game and elevated him to heights he didn't know he was capable of. With Crunch trudging along beside him selecting clubs for him and pointing out the proper places to aim and reading all the greens, Townsend played the finest round of his life. The wind blew hard off the sea, as it is supposed to do at North Berwick, and rain showers struck a couple of times, but Townsend marched bravely through the elements and holed a birdie putt at the eighteenth to finish two over par.

Townsend gave Crunch a handsome tip and arranged to meet him at the North Berwick golf shop the next morning for the beginning of the tournament.

"Do you know this fellow called Liam Flaherty?" Townsend asked the caddie.

"Aye," said Crunch.

"Tell me about him," Townsend said.

"Ah, he's no good," replied Crunch in his East Lothian dialect. "He's no good with his driver. He's no good with his irons. He's no good with his putter. He's just flat no good at all."

Townsend beamed at this news. "Flaherty is my opponent in the first round tomorrow."

"Ah," said Crunch. "He'll beat you."'

HARVEY PENICK – FROM *THE GAME FOR A LIFETIME* (1996)

JONES'S RULES AND ONE MORE

'Bobby Jones said because tension is golf's worst enemy, he had set forth six rules that would help develop a freewheeling swing.

    1. Grip the club lightly, mainly in the fingers, and make sure you can feel the clubhead.

    2. In addressing the ball, arrange your posture as naturally and comfortably as possible.

    3. Use the legs and hips in beginning the backswing, and swing the club back rather than picking it up with the hands and arms.

    4. Be sure your backswing is long enough that your downswing will have time to get up speed before contact.

    5. Start your downswing in a leisurely fashion, in no hurry coming down, with the acceleration smooth and natural.

    6. When it comes time to hit, don't leap at the ball, but keep on swinging until the ball has had a good start down the fairway, and the clubhead has done its job.

To these rules, I would add one more for the average golfer – be sure your shoulders are square to the line.'

IBID.

'IN 1776 Lieutenant James Dalrymple was fined six pints of beer by golfers of the Honourable Company of Edinburgh for having five times played at Leith Golf Club without wearing the club's uniform, thereby breaching the regulations. The uniform consisted of a red jacket bearing the club's crest, black tie, white shirt and buff knee-breeches. Clearly, strange dress was as much a feature of the game two hundred years ago as it is today.'

Bride: 'Whatever made you bring your silly old golf clubs to our wedding?'
Groom: 'Well, it's not going to take all day, is it?'
ANON.

'Smith sliced his ball from the fifth tee and it narrowly missed the head of a friend on the ninth fairway. "I shouted 'Fore!' old man, why didn't you duck? I might have killed you."
"It wouldn't have mattered a damn," said his friend, "I took thirteen at the last hole."'
TERRY HALL

'A member of the United States Walker Cup team, Charley Yates, from Atlanta, fought his way through the 1938 British Amateur and beat the Irishman Cecil Ewing by 3 and 2 in the final match, at Troon. The championship won, Yates asked a Scottish friend to send a telegram to his boss in Atlanta announcing his victory. A modest and succinct man, Yates sent two words. The message read: "Fortune smiled."'
ROBERT T. SOMMERS – FROM *GOLF ANECDOTES*

HELL BUNKER

'While it has been relatively stable throughout the twentieth century, the Old Course at St Andrews evolved over a long period of years. Hell Bunker, a deep and wide depression about 80 yards short of the fourteenth green, began as a much smaller obstacle in 1882, while Old Tom Morris served in the dual position of professional to the R and A [Royal and Ancient] and greenkeeper of the course.

One day an indignant golfer fumed to Morris that the condition of the course was so bad he had had only one decent lie all day, and that was at the bottom of Hell Bunker. His ball lay so well, he was able to play a wooden club from it.

Morris's features, usually dark in their normal state, turned black. Immediately he sent a work crew to the site armed with picks and hoes and had them hack away until no golfer could ever again play from Hell Bunker with a wood . . . '

IBID.

'A golf professional, hired by a big department store to give golf lessons to interested customers, was approached by two ladies.

"Do you wish to learn to play golf, madam?" he asked one of them.

"Oh no," she replied, "it's my friend here who's interested. I learnt last Wednesday."'

– FROM *REALLY WICKED GOLF JOKES*

'After a particularly poor game of golf, a popular club member skipped the clubhouse and started to go home. As he was walking to the car park to get to his car, a policeman stopped him and asked, "Did you tee off on the sixteenth hole about twenty minutes ago?"

"Yes," replied the golfer.

"Did you happen to hook the ball so that it went over the trees and off the course?" asked the policeman.

"Yes, I did. How did you know?" the golfer asked.

"Well," said the policeman in a serious tone of voice, "your ball flew out on to the road and crashed through a driver's windscreen. The car went out of control, crashing into five other cars and a fire engine. The fire engine couldn't make it to the fire and the building burned down. So what are you going to do about it?"

The golfer thought it over carefully and responded, "I think I'll close my stance a little bit, tighten my grip and lower my right thumb."'

Ibid.

"'Why don't you play golf with Captain Fortescue any more, John?" the young wife enquired.

"Well, would you play golf with a man who talks while you're playing, fiddles his score and moves his ball out of the rough when you're not looking?"

"Certainly not!"

"Neither will the Captain."'

– FROM *The World's Best Golf Jokes*

"'My wife says that if I don't give up golf she'll leave me."

"Say, that's tough, old man."

"Yes, I'm going to miss her."'

Ibid.

"'Mildred, shut up," cried the golfer at his nagging wife. "Shut up or you'll drive me out of my mind."

"That," snapped Mildred, "that wouldn't be a drive. That would be a putt."'

Ibid.

'Sam and Janet were beginning a game of golf. Janet stepped up to the tee, and her first drive gave her a hole in one. Sam stepped

up to the tee and said, "OK, now I'll just take *my* practice swing, and then we'll start the game."'
IBID.

'Golfers are said to be eternal pessimists – witness the man who walked on to the first tee, took a practice swing, tore up his card and went home.'
TOM O'CONNOR

'The scent of the conifers, sound of the bath,
The view from my bedroom of moss-dappled path,
As I struggle with double-end evening tie,
For we dance at the Golf Club, my victor and I . . . '
JOHN BETJEMAN – FROM 'A SUBALTERN'S LOVE-SONG'

'I was playing golf
The day the Germans landed;
All our troops had run away,
All our ships were stranded.
And the thought of England's shame
Altogether spoiled my game.'
HARRY GRAHAM – FROM *MORE RUTHLESS RHYMES*

'Many a heart is aching
If you could read them all,
Many the hopes that have vanished,
After the ball . . . '
CHARLES K. HARRIS – FROM 'AFTER THE BALL'

# NOVEL
# EXTRACTS

*(Julian Barnes's life-after-death fantasy envisages a truly celestial golf course . . . )*

'Let me start with the golf. Now, I've never been much good at the game, but I used to enjoy hacking round a municipal course where the grass is like coconut matting and no one bothers to replace their divots because there are so many holes in the fairway you can't work out where your divot has come from anyway. Still, I'd seen most of the famous courses on television and I was curious to play – well, the golf of my dreams. And as soon as I felt the contact my driver made on that first tee and watched the ball howling off a couple of hundred yards, I knew I was in seventh heaven. My clubs seemed perfectly weighted to the touch; the fairways had a lush springiness and held the ball up for you like a waiter with a drinks tray; and my caddy (I'd never had a caddy before, but he treated me like Arnold Palmer) was full of useful advice, never pushy. The course seemed to have everything – streams and lakes and antique bridges, bits of seaside links like in Scotland, patches of flowering dogwood and azalea from Augusta, beechwood, pine, bracken and gorse. It was a difficult course, but one that gave you chances. I went round that sunny morning in sixty-seven, which was five under par, and twenty shots better than I'd ever done on the municipal course.'

JULIAN BARNES – FROM *A HISTORY OF THE WORLD IN $10^{1}/_{2}$ CHAPTERS*

*(On the trail of a nest of spies, John Buchan's hero runs across an
unlikely looking trio of 'traitors'.)*

'Presently a third figure arrived, a young man on a bicycle with a bag
of golf clubs slung on his back. He strolled round to the tennis lawn
and was welcomed riotously by the players. Evidently they were
chaffing him, and their chaff sounded horribly English. Then the
plump man, mopping his brow with a silk handerkerchief, announced
that he must have a tub. I heard his very words – "I've got into a
proper lather," he said. "This will bring down my weight and my
handicap, Bob. I'll take you on tomorrow and give you a stroke a
hole." You couldn't find anything much more English than that.

They went into the house, and left me feeling a precious idiot. I
had been barking up the wrong tree all this time. These men might
be acting; but if they were, where was their audience? They didn't
know I was sitting thirty yards off in a rhododendron. It was
simply impossible to believe that these three hearty fellows were
anything but what they seemed – three ordinary, game-playing,
suburban Englishmen, wearisome, if you like, but solidly
innocent.'

JOHN BUCHAN – FROM *THE THIRTY-NINE STEPS*

*(After renting a house on Long Island next door to the mysterious Jay
Gatsby, Scott Fitzgerald's narrator, Nick Carraway, falls in with a
wealthy, fashionable crowd, including Jordan Baker, society beauty and
golfing champion . . . )*

'For a while I lost sight of Jordan Baker, and then in midsummer I
found her again. At first I was flattered to go places with her
because she was a golf champion and everyone knew her name.
Then it was something more. I wasn't actually in love, but I felt a

sort of tender curiosity. The bored haughty face that she turned to
the world concealed something – most affectations conceal
something eventually, even though they don't in the beginning –
and one day I found what it was. When we were on a house party
together up in Warwick, she left a borrowed car out in the rain
with the top down, and then lied about it – and suddenly I
remembered the story about her that had eluded me that night at
Daisy's. At her first big golf tournament there was a row that
nearly reached the newspapers – a suggestion that she had moved
her ball from a bad lie in the semi-final round. The thing
approached the proportions of a scandal – then died away. A caddy
retracted his statement and the only other witness admitted that he
might have been mistaken. The incident and the name had
remained together in my mind.'

F. SCOTT FITZGERALD – FROM *THE GREAT GATSBY*

*(When the body of eccentric millionaire P. T. Renauld is discovered on the
golf course adjoining his mansion in the French countryside, Agatha
Christie's celebrated sleuth, Hercule Poirot, is called upon to investigate . . . )*

'"Why, this is a golf course," I cried.

Bex nodded.

"The links are not completed yet," he explained. "It is hoped to
be able to open them some time next month. It was some of the
men working on them who discovered the body early this
morning."

I gave a gasp. A little to my left, where for the moment I had
overlooked it, was a long narrow pit and by it, face down, was the
body of a man! For a moment my heart gave a terrible leap, and I
had a wild fancy that the tragedy had been duplicated. But the
commissary dispelled my illusion by moving forward with a sharp
exclamation of annoyance:

"What have my police been about? They had strict orders to allow no one near the place without proper credentials!"

The man on the ground turned his head over his shoulder.

"But I have proper credentials," he remarked, and rose slowly to his feet.

"My dear Monsieur Giraud," cried the commissary. "I had no idea you had arrived, even. The examining magistrate has been awaiting you with the utmost impatience."

As he spoke, I was scanning the newcomer with the keenest curiosity. The famous detective from the Paris Sûreté was familiar to me by name, and I was extremely interested to see him in the flesh. He was very tall, perhaps about thirty years of age, with auburn hair and moustache, and a military carriage. There was a trace of arrogance in his manner which showed he was fully alive to his own importance. Bex introduced us, presenting Poirot as a colleague. A flicker of interest came into the detective's eye.

"I know you by name, Monsieur Poirot," he said. "You cut quite a figure in the old days, didn't you? But methods are very different now."

"Crimes, though, are very much the same," remarked Poirot gently.

I saw at once that Giraud was prepared to be hostile. He resented the other being associated with him, and I felt that if he came across any clue of importance he would be more than likely to keep it to himself.

"The examining magistrate – " began Bex again.

But Giraud interrupted rudely:

"A fig for the examining magistrate! The light is the important thing. For all practical purposes it will be gone in another half-hour or so. I know all about the case, and the people at the house will do very well until tomorrow; but if we're going to find a clue to the murderers, here is the spot we shall find it. Is it your police who have been trampling all over the place? I thought they knew better nowadays."

"Assuredly they do. The marks you complain of were made by the workmen who discovered the body."

The other grunted disgustedly.

"I can see the tracks where the three of them came through the hedge – but they were cunning. You can just recognize the centre footmarks as those of Monsieur Renauld, but those on either side have been carefully obliterated. Not that there would have been much to see anyway on this hard ground, but they weren't taking any chances."

"The external sign," said Poirot. "That is what you seek, eh?"

The other detective stared.

"Of course."

A very faint smile came to Poirot's lips. He seemed about to speak, but checked himself. He bent down to where a spade was lying.

"That's what the grave was dug with, right enough," said Giraud. "But you'll get nothing from it. It was Renauld's own spade, and the man who used it wore gloves. Here they are." He gesticulated with his foot to where two soil-stained gloves were lying. "And they're Renauld's too – or at least his gardener's. I tell you, the men who planned out this crime were taking no chances. The man was stabbed with his own dagger, and would have been buried with his own spade. They counted on leaving no traces! But I'll beat them. There's always *something*. And I mean to find it."

But Poirot was now apparently interested in something else, a short, discoloured piece of lead piping which lay beside the spade. He touched it delicately with his finger.

"And does this, too, belong to the murdered man?" he asked, and I thought I detected a subtle flavour of irony in the question.

Giraud shrugged his shoulders to indicate that he neither knew nor cared.

"May have been lying around here for weeks. Anyway, it doesn't interest me."

"I, on the contrary, find it very interesting," said Poirot sweetly.

I guessed that he was merely bent on annoying the Paris detective and, if so, he succeeded. The other turned away rudely, remarking that he had no time to waste, and bending down he resumed his minute search of the ground.

Meanwhile, Poirot, as though struck by a sudden idea, stepped back over the boundary, and tried the door of the little shed.

"That's locked," said Giraud over his shoulder. "But it's only a place where the gardener keeps his rubbish. The spade didn't come from there, but from the tool-shed up by the house."

"Marvellous," murmured M. Bex ecstatically to me. "He has been here but half an hour, and he already knows everything! What a man! Undoubtedly Giraud is the greatest detective alive today."

Although I disliked the detective heartily, I nevertheless was secretly impressed. Efficiency seemed to radiate from the man. I could not help feeling that, so far, Poirot had not greatly distinguished himself, and it vexed me. He seemed to be directing his attention to all sorts of silly puerile points that had nothing to do with the case. Indeed, at this juncture, he suddenly asked:

"Monsieur Bex, tell me, I pray you, the meaning of this white-washed line that extends all around the grave. Is it a device of the police?"

"No, Monsieur Poirot, it is an affair of the golf course. It shows that there is here to be a 'bunkair', as you call it."

"A bunkair?" Poirot turned to me. "That is the irregular hole filled with sand and a bank at one side, is it not?"

I concurred.

"Monsieur Renauld, without doubt he played the golf?"

"Yes, he was a keen golfer. It's mainly owing to him, and to his large subscriptions, that this work is being carried forward. He even had a say in the designing of it."

Poirot nodded thoughtfully. Then he remarked:

"It was not a very good choice they made – of a spot to bury the body? When the men began to dig up the ground, all would have been discovered."

"Exactly," cried Giraud triumphantly. "And that *proves* that they were strangers to the place. It's an excellent piece of indirect evidence."

"Yes," said Poirot doubtfully. "No one who knew would bury a body there – unless they wanted it to be discovered. And that is clearly absurd, is it not?"

Giraud did not even trouble to reply.

"Yes," said Poirot, in a somewhat dissatisfied voice. "Yes – undoubtedly – absurd!'"

AGATHA CHRISTIE – FROM *THE MURDER ON THE LINKS*

*(After a series of mysterious 'accidents' and sabotage attempts – including the theft of a putter – fail to stop him from taking part in the competition, a young British golfing champion plays the first round of the Ryder Cup.)*

'I handed the new club to Ben who eyed it suspiciously, as well he might. I knew that he had used the same putter for several years. It was an old and trusted friend to him and now, in the most important match of his young career, he had to strike up an acquaintance with an alien being. Ben gripped it, lined it up on the tee and swung it tentatively. To my relief he said, "It feels fine, it'll be fine."

The Blackstocks were still stationed by the tee and I spotted Suzi in the crowd just behind them. I looked back at the crowd as we moved off the tee and had my first sighting of the religious fanatic who is often seen at major American tournaments and who always manages to get his banner into camera shot. On this occasion the banner read, "Genesis IV 10" I wondered what it meant but didn't have a bible on me to check the quotation.

Ben's swing, as graceful and steady as anyone could wish,

propelled his ball on to the green but Farrell, unperturbed, put his ball to within ten feet of the hole. Ben had twice that distance to go, downhill across a left to right slope. This was a feel putt if ever there was one and I prayed that the putter would work well for him and inspire him with confidence. The stroke was slow and smooth and Ben's ball started down the slope and, halfway to the hole, began to turn. It wavered slightly as it hit a spike mark and then continued on its course and dropped neatly into the hole.

"What a lovely putter," Ben said quietly. Farrell missed his easier putt by several inches. We were one hole up and in good heart. I nudged Ben as we stood on the second tee and nodded at the scoreboard. Nick Spencer was three in the lead after fourteen holes and Gonzales was two up. Europe was ahead in five other matches and only behind in two. The prospects were good and even better when Ben sank a putt of around twelve feet to take a two-hole lead.

There have been many remarkable matches in the Ryder Cup, great golfing deeds accomplished in the fury of battle, but the quality of golf produced by Ben Massey and Jerry Farrell can rarely have been surpassed. Like the doughty battler he is, Farrell hit back with two birdies and an eagle of his own in the next few holes to go one ahead of Ben and, at the halfway mark, the match was level. Between them the players had notched up six birdies and two eagles.

As the spectators realized that a battle royal had been joined they began to desert the other matches to join in the fun. The atmosphere was tense enough at the start and the swelling crowd, stretched twenty or more deep down the fairways and clinging to every vantage point, rushing frantically from green to green, made me feel almost claustrophobic.

On the tenth tee the scoreboard told us that both Nick Spencer and Ramon Gonzales had won their matches. Even more encouraging was that Dan Appleby had fought his way back to halve the match. As Ben prepared for his tee shot I saw the scoreboard change again and a great cheer went up from the European fans; Dave Curran had also snatched half a point in his match.

Ben hit yet another solid drive down the tenth fairway; the ball was crunching off the middle of his club. As he gave me his driver I nodded at the scorebord. "We're only one point behind. Bentley's prayers are being answered."

"Yeah, well, keep praying. Perhaps we need that guy's help, too." Ben gestured at the bearded man of God with the placard; he had managed to worm his way to the front of the spectators again.

The initial fury of the two contestants' exchanges had now calmed and they managed to halve the next holes in straightforward, even docile, fashion. But the American team were far from finished; Mike Dolby and Luis Moreno were both defeated but this was relieved by the news that Jose Miguel had beaten Curtis Sawyer by a two-hole margin.

On the thirteenth tee we were joined by Toby. "Keep going, Chris. The Americans need two points from the last five matches to win."

Farrell responded to this information by making birdies at the next two holes but Ben kept the match level with two of his own at the fourteenth and fifteenth holes.

On the next tee a huge wave of cheering rent the air as Tony Swan beat John Brady on the final green and the noise multiplied as Stefan Sandberg's victory over Larry Sussman was flashed up on the scoreboards.

"We're level in the whole match, for the first time," said Ben.

Such equilibrium did not last because Travis Hanson registered a narrow win over Ernst Tillman, just when Ben and Farrell halved the short sixteenth with par threes.

By this time the whole crowd had compressed itself between the seventeenth and eighteenth holes. The Americans needed one point to win the Ryder Cup whereas the European team required both points for victory. Ahead, we knew that Jack Mason was one hole in the lead against Jeff Malton.

On the seventeenth tee I caught sight of Suzi, squashed between two broad-beamed Americans, both of whom were carrying cans of beer. She gave me a thumbs up and all I could do was gulp and smile weakly back. Both Ben and Farrell successfully threaded their drives between the menacing fairway bunkers. This was no time for heroics and they both hit irons conservatively to the centre of the green.

By this time Ross Bentley had joined us and, as the two golfers conscientiously holed out for their par fours, he walked with us to the final tee, his radio to his ear. "Malton's missed his birdie putt," Bentley muttered to us. "Jack's conceded the par four. He's got a putt of thirty feet. Oh God, I'm glad I don't have to face those shots any more."

Bentley was sweating heavily and his knuckles were white around the radio. "It's on its way," he said. A great cheer came rolling back from the eighteenth green and then it changed to a deep groan.

We had reached the tee but, owing to the undulations of the ground, could only see the bobbing heads of the players, the caddies and the various officials. "He's four feet past," Bentley muttered. Although he was sweating, his face looked grey. "If he misses . . . "

The various permutations flashed through my mind. Two halved matches meant a win for the United States, but the win and a half meant a tied match and, as the holders, Europe would retain the trophy. Not a satisfactory outcome and certainly not the sort of negative thought to plant in Ben's mind. My analysis was checked by another great roar from the crowd around the eighteenth and we could see a forest of arms waving.

"He's done it," shouted Ross Bentley. "He's done it."

"Come on, Ben," I said quietly. "We need a birdie."

He nodded and smiled. The crowd were eerily silent and the only sounds I registered were the slight sighing of the wind and the discreet flapping of a flag on a nearby green. Ben adjusted the glove on his left hand, ran his right hand through his hair, took a deep breath and addressed his ball.

Ross Bentley was shielding his eyes and looking away up the rolling fairway. Toby, who as a journalist was allowed inside the ropes, deliberately turned his head away as Ben began his swing. In the circumstances his shot deserved the applause it received. The ball landed on the right side of the fairway and was well beyond the ridge which runs across the fairway just over 200 yards from the tee and menaces the drives of less gifted golfers. The only problem which I perceived was that a high mound cut into the fairway just ahead of Ben's ball and might well interfere with the line of his shot to the green.

"Bread-and-butter drive," Ben muttered, "when I need Sunday roast."

Farrell produced the latter and his ball finished in the left centre of the fairway, about thirty yards beyond Ben's.

The crowd stampeded down the edges of the fairway and, followed by Ross Bentley and the American captain, Tony Bendix, in their respective buggies, we trudged towards Ben's ball.

As I feared, the mound, cunningly placed by the designer, prevented Ben from hitting a direct shot to the green. He walked back and forth trying to assess the angles. Since the hole had been cut, once again, on the left edge of the plateau green, I knew that Ben had been planning to draw his second shot from right to left in order to get close to the flag.

"I daren't risk a draw," he said. "I'd have to go over the highest point of the mound. It'll have to be the fade. How far to the pin?"

"Hundred and ninety yards."

"Four-iron, then."

The marshals had moved the crowd away from the slopes of the mound with great difficulty and that unnerving silence settled again over the crowd as Ben fidgeted into his stance. The safe shot was a left to right fade to the centre of the green; but if Ben aspired to a birdie he had to flirt perilously with the deep bunkers in order to land the ball on the left edge of the green.

The rhythm and stability of Ben's swing and the healthy smack of iron on balata told me that he had made a perfect contact. The line of the shot told me that Ben had gone for broke and the ball ripped through the air towards the bunkers on the left of the green. It should turn at any moment as the spin took effect, and so it did.

My fingers were digging into my palms as I watched, Ben motionless beside me. Thump went the ball into the edge of the green and I waited for its roll down the slope towards the hole. The ball hovered for a moment and then rolled slowly and inexorably off the edge of the green into the bunker. The misjudgement had been only a matter of a few inches but I knew that Ben would be seen, despite all his heroics on the previous two days, as the man who lost the Ryder Cup for Europe.

The British spectators were silent while the Americans mixed shouts of delight with sympathetic applause. Ross Bentley held his head in his hands in anguish. Without expression on his taut face, Ben stared at the ground.

Jerry Farrell, relieved of any necessity to try and make a birdie, hit a smooth shot to the centre of the green. Tony Bendix jumped off his buggy and embraced his player and Farrell acknowledged the thundering cries of congratulations from his fans.

When we reached Ben's ball in the bunker I knew that he would be fortunate to play it out to within twenty feet of a hole which was no more than fifteen feet from the edge of the deep and steeply faced bunker. Not only that but the green ran sharply downhill from Ben and there was a noticeable borrow from left to right. My mind wound itself back to memories of the unfortunate Tommy Nakajima who, in the Open Championship, had taken four shots to extricate his ball from a bunker at the infamous road hole at St Andrews. Ben's shot looked even more difficult.

Since Farrell's ball lay further from the hole, he putted first and laid it to rest no more than a foot from the pin. Ben conceded his par four and, with a broad smile, Farrell threw his ball into the crowd. The applause went on and on; to all intents and purposes the Ryder Cup had returned to America for the first time for a decade. Stewards and officials, and Farrell himself, gestured the crowd into silence and Ben prepared to play a shot whose immense difficulty had been magnified by its circumstances.

With no margin for error, Ben had to cut the ball steeply into the

air and try and land it on the edge of the green. If he played the
shot perfectly, there was a chance that the ball might stop within ten
feet of the hole, but the slope of the green was so severe that I
thought such a result unlikely. There was a real danger that Ben
would not even get the ball out of the bunker, so close was he to its
face.

We looked one last time at the line of the shot and tried to
compute the effect of the spin which Ben would impart with the
open face of his sand-wedge, and the speed and angle of the slope.

Ben stepped back into the sand and said, "OK, it's got to go in. I
wish I'd gone to Stefan's prayer meetings now. Will you hold the flag
for me, please, Chris."

As I stood with the flagstick in my hand, I could just see the top
of Ben's head. Tens of thousands of people around the green were
craning their necks to witness the final throes of the drama. All the
players, the two captains and the officials of both teams were
scattered around the edges of the green. Ross Bentley had his head
in his hands again; and Stefan Sandberg had his hands clasped
together, in prayer, I hoped. I wondered whether my mother and
father were watching on television.

In total silence, Ben took one more look over the edge of the
bunker and then I saw his club as it reached the top of its arc. The
swing was slow and smooth, Ben's head motionless. As long as the
ball comes out, we've got a chance, I thought. A putt for a half to tie
the scores and the Ryder Cup stays in Europe.

I watched intently as the clubhead began its downwards journey; I
heard a sort of whoosh as contact was made with the sand; and then
everything went into slow motion as a shower of sand came over the
edge of the bunker followed by Ben's ball. Out it came, steeply up
into the sky, spinning, spinning. I swore later that I was able to count
its every revolution and even read the maker's name. An American
writer once compared the flight of a golf ball to man's aspirations
for immortality; in those moments, as I stood waiting on the
eighteenth green at Eagle Cliffs, I think I understood what he meant.

The ball pitched about four feet from the edge of the green, jumped in the air and began to roll across and down the slope. As the spin imparted by Ben's sand-iron ceased the ball began to gather pace. It couldn't possibly stop anywhere near the hole, I knew it was going to miss on my right; I removed the flag and stood back. When it was eighteen inches away I thought the ball would hit the edge of the hole and spin away down the slope. It was rolling even faster but took one more slight turn across the slope and with a clunk, the ball hit the back of the hole, jumped in the air and then settled in the bottom of the cup. A birdie – victory! Glory for Ben and a surge of delight for me.

Ben came hurtling on to the green, flung his arms around me and danced us both around the green. I saw Jerry Farrell, who had played superbly throughout the match, with shoulders slumped and head down. I remember very little after that except that we were engulfed by the European players and officials, and by the fans. Ross Bentley and Ben were carried shoulder high from the eighteenth green and hordes of journalists and radio and television interviewers were bellowing questions at Ben, at Ross, at anybody connected with the European team.

You couldn't hear let alone think straight in the hubbub and confusion, and champagne corks were popping like toy machine guns. Someone grabbed me around the shoulders and shoved a bottle in my hands and I drank deeply, the lovely nectar bubbling and foaming over my face and down my shirt. Ben upended a bottle over my head and amid a scrum of people, shouting and cheering and clapping us on the backs, we eventually reached the sanctuary of the clubhouse.'

MALCOLM HAMER – FROM *DEATH TRAP*

*(Ian Fleming's debonair secret agent, 007, takes on the sinister Goldfinger in a 'sudden-death' match . . .)*

'Goldfinger had already teed up. Bond walked slowly behind him, followed by Hawker. Bond stood and leant on his driver. He said, "I thought you said we would be playing the strict rules of golf. But I'll give you that putt. That makes you one up."

Goldfinger nodded curtly. He went through his practice routine and hit his usual excellent, safe drive.

The second hole is a three-hundred-and-seventy-yard dogleg to the left with deep cross-bunkers daring you to take the tiger's line. But there was a light helping breeze. For Goldfinger it would now be a five iron for his second. Bond decided to try and make it easier for himself and only have a wedge for the green. He laid his ears back and hit the ball hard and straight for the bunkers. The breeze got under the slight draw and winged the ball on and over. The ball pitched and disappeared down into the gully just short of the green. A four. Chance of a three.

Goldfinger strode off without comment. Bond lengthened his stride and caught up. "How's the agoraphobia? Doesn't all this wide open space bother it?"

"No."

Goldfinger deviated to the right. He glanced at the distant, half-hidden flag planning his second shot. He took his five iron and hit a good, careful shot which took a bad kick short of the green and ran down into the thick grass to the left. Bond knew the territory. Goldfinger would be lucky to get down in two.

Bond walked up to his ball, took the wedge and flicked the ball on to the green with plenty of stop. The ball pulled up and lay a yard past the hole. Goldfinger executed a creditable pitch but missed the twelve-foot putt. Bond had two for the hole from a yard. He didn't wait to be given the hole but walked up and putted. The ball stopped an inch short. Goldfinger walked off the green. Bond knocked the ball in. All square.

The third is a blind two hundred and forty yards, all carry, a difficult three. Bond chose his brassie and hit a good one. It would be on or near the green. Goldfinger's routine drive was well hit but would probably not have enough steam to carry the last of the rough and trickle down into the saucer of the green. Sure enough, Goldfinger's ball was on top of the protecting mound of rough. He had a nasty, cuppy lie, with a tuft just behind the ball. Goldfinger stopped and looked at the lie. He seemed to make up his mind. He stepped past his ball to take a club from the caddie. His left foot came down just behind the ball, flattening the tuft. Goldfinger could now take his putter. He did so and trickled the ball down the bank towards the hole. It stopped three feet short.

Bond frowned. The only remedy against a cheat at golf is not to play with him again. But that was no good in this match. Bond had no intention of playing with the man again. And it was no good starting a you-did-I-didn't argument unless he caught Goldfinger doing something even more outrageous. Bond would just have to try and beat him, cheating and all.

Now Bond's twenty-foot putt was no joke. There was no question of going for the hole. He would have to concentrate on laying it dead. As usual when one plays to go dead, the ball stopped short – a good yard short. Bond took a lot of trouble about the putt and holed it, sweating. He knocked Goldfinger's ball away. He would go on giving Goldfinger missable putts until suddenly Bond would ask him to hole one. Then that one might look just a bit more difficult.

Still all square. The fourth is four hundred and sixty yards. You drive over one of the tallest and deepest bunkers in the United Kingdom and then have a long second shot across an undulating hilly fairway to a plateau green guarded by a final steep slope which makes it easier to take three putts than two.

Bond picked up his usual fifty yards on the drive and Goldfinger hit two of his respectable shots to the gully below the green. Bond, determined to get up, took a brassie instead of a spoon and went over to the green and almost up against the boundary fence. From there he was glad to get down in three for a half.

The fifth was again a long carry, followed by Bond's favourite second shot on the course – over bunkers and through a valley between high sand-dunes to a distant, taunting flag. It is a testing hole for which the first essential is a well-placed drive. Bond stood on the tee, perched high up in the sand-hills, and paused before the shot while he gazed at the glittering distant sea and at the faraway crescent of cliffs beyond Pegwell Bay. Then he took up his stance and visualized the tennis court of turf that was his target. He took the club back as slowly as he knew how and started down for the last terrific acceleration before the club head met the ball. There was a dull clang on his right. It was too late to stop. Desperately Bond focused the ball and tried to keep his swing all in one piece. There came the ugly clonk of a mis-hit ball. Bond's head shot up. It was a lofted hook. Would it have the legs? Get on! Get on! The ball hit the top of a mountain of rough and bounced over. Would it reach the beginning of the fairway?

Bond turned towards Goldfinger and the caddies, his eyes fierce. Goldfinger was straightening up. He met Bond's eye indifferently. "Sorry. Dropped my driver."

"Don't do it again," Bond said curtly. He stood down off the tee and handed his driver to Hawker. Hawker shook his head sympathetically. Bond took out a cigarette and lit it. Goldfinger hit his drive the dead straight regulation two hundred yards.

They walked down the hill in silence which Goldfinger unexpectedly broke. "What is the firm you work for?"

"Universal Export."

"And where do they hang out?"

"London. Regent's Park."

"What do they export?"

Bond woke up from his angry ruminations. Here, pay attention! This is work, not a game. All right, he put you off your drive, but you've got your cover to think about. Don't let him needle you into making mistakes about it. Build up the story. Bond said casually, "Oh, everything from sewing-machines to tanks."

"What's your speciality?"

Bond could feel Goldfinger's eyes on him. He said, "I look after the small-arms side. Spend most of my time selling miscellaneous ironmongery to sheiks and rajahs – anyone the Foreign Office decides doesn't want the stuff to shoot at us."

"Interesting work." Goldfinger's voice was flat, bored.

"Not very. I'm thinking of quitting. Came down here for a week's holiday to think it out. Not much future in England. Rather like the idea of Canada."

"Indeed?"

They were past the rough and Bond was relieved to find that his ball had got a forward kick off the hill on to the fairway. The fairway curved slightly to the left and Bond had even managed to pick up a few feet on Goldfinger. It was Goldfinger to play. Goldfinger took out his spoon. He wasn't going for the green but only to get over the bunkers and through the valley.

Bond waited for the usual safe shot. He looked at his own lie. Yes, he could take his brassie. There came the wooden thud of a mis-hit. Goldfinger's ball, hit off the heel, sped along the ground and into the stony wastes of Hell Bunker – the widest bunker and the only unkempt one, because of the pebbles, on the course.

For once Homer had nodded – or rather, lifted his head. Perhaps his mind had been half on what Bond had told him. Good show! But Goldfinger might still get down in three more. Bond took out his brassie. He couldn't afford to play safe. He addressed the ball, seeing in his mind's eye the eighty-eight-millimetre trajectory through the valley and then the two or three bounces that would take it on to the green. He laid off a bit to the right to allow for his draw. Now!

There came a soft clinking away to his right. Bond stood away from his ball. Goldfinger had his back to Bond. He was gazing out to sea, rapt in its contemplation, while his right hand played "unconsciously" with the money in his pocket.

Bond smiled grimly. He said, "Could you stop shifting bullion till after my shot?"

Goldfinger didn't answer or turn round. The noise stopped.

Bond turned back to his shot, desperately trying to clear his mind again. Now the brassie was too much of a risk. It needed too good a shot. He handed it to Hawker and took his spoon and banged the ball safely through the valley. It ran on well and stopped on the apron. A five, perhaps a four.

Goldfinger got well out of the bunker and put his chip dead. Bond putted too hard and missed the one back. Still all square.

The sixth, apppropriately called "The Virgin", is a famous short hole in the world of golf. A narrow green, almost ringed with bunkers, it can need anything from an eight to a two iron according to the wind. Today for Bond, it was a seven. He played a soaring shot, laid off to the right for the wind to bring it in. It ended twenty feet beyond the pin with a difficult putt over and down a shoulder. Should be a three. Goldfinger took his five and played it straight. The breeze took it and it rolled into the deep bunker on the left. Good news! That would be the hell of a difficult three.

They walked in silence to the green. Bond glanced into the bunker. Goldfinger's ball was in a deep heel-mark. Bond walked over to his ball and listened to the larks. This was going to put him one up. He looked for Hawker to take his putter, but Hawker was on the other side of the green, watching with intent concentration Goldfinger play his shot. Goldfinger got down into the bunker with his blaster. He jumped up to get a view of the hole and then settled himself for the shot. As his club went up Bond's heart lifted. He was going to try and flick it out – a hopeless technique from that buried lie. The only hope would have been to explode it. Down came the club, smoothly, without hurry. With hardly a handful of sand the ball curved up out of the deep bunker, bounced once and lay dead!

Bond swallowed. Blast his eyes! How the hell had Goldfinger

managed that? Now, out of sour grapes, Bond must try for his two. He went for it, missed the hole by an inch and rolled a good yard past. Hell and damnation! Bond walked slowly up to the putt, knocking Goldfinger's ball away. Come on, you bloody fool! But the spectre of the big swing – from an almost certain one up to a possible one down – made Bond wish the ball into the hole instead of tapping it in. The coaxed ball, lacking decision, slid past the lip. One down!

Now Bond was angry with himself. He, and he alone, had lost that hole. He had taken three putts from twenty feet. He really must pull himself together and get going.

At the seventh, five hundred yards, they both hit good drives and Goldfinger's immaculate second lay fifty yards short of the green. Bond took his brassie. Now for the equalizer! But he hit from the top, his club head came down too far ahead of the hands and the smothered ball shot into one of the right-hand bunkers. Not a good lie, but he must put it on the green. Bond took a dangerous seven and failed to get out. Goldfinger got his five. Two down. They halved the short eighth in three. At the ninth Bond, determined to turn only one down, again tried to do too much off a poor lie. Goldfinger got his four to Bond's five. Three down at the turn! Not too good. Bond asked Hawker for a new ball. Hawker unwrapped it slowly, waiting for Goldfinger to walk over the hillock to the next tee. Hawker said softly, "You saw what he did at the Virgin, sir?"

"Yes, damn him. It was an amazing shot."

Hawker was surprised. "Oh, you didn't see what he did in the bunker, sir?"

"No, what? I was too far away."

The other two were out of sight over the rise. Hawker silently walked down into one of the bunkers guarding the ninth green, kicked a hole with his toe and dropped the ball in the hole. He then stood just behind the half-buried ball with his feet close together. He looked up at Bond. "Remember he jumped up to look at the line to the hole, sir?"

"Yes."

"Just watch this, sir." Hawker looked towards the ninth pin and jumped, just as Goldfinger had done, as if to get the line. Then he looked up at Bond again and pointed to the ball at his feet. The heavy impact of the two feet just behind the ball had levelled the hole in which it had lain and had squeezed the ball out so that it was now perfectly teed for an easy shot – for just the easy cut-up shot which had seemed utterly impossible from Goldfinger's lie at the Virgin.

Bond looked at his caddie for a moment in silence. Then he said, "Thanks, Hawker. Give me the bat and the ball. Somebody's going to be second in this match, and I'm damned if it's going to be me."

"Yes, sir," said Hawker stolidly. He limped off on the short cut that would take him half way down the tenth fairway.

Bond sauntered slowly over the rise and down to the tenth tee. He hardly looked at Goldfinger who was standing on the tee swishing his driver impatiently. Bond was clearing his mind of everything but cold, offensive resolve. For the first time since the first tee he felt supremely confident. All he needed was a sign from Heaven and his game would catch fire.

The tenth at the Royal St Mark's is the most dangerous hole on the course. The second shot, to the skiddy plateau green with cavernous bunkers to right and left and a steep hill beyond, has broken many hearts. Bond remembered that Philip Scrutton, out in four under fours in the Gold Bowl, had taken a fourteen at this hole, seven of them ping-pong shots from one bunker to another, to and fro across the green. Bond knew that Goldfinger would play his second to the apron, or short of it, and would be glad to get a five. Bond must go for it and get his four.

Two good drives and, sure enough, Goldfinger well up on the apron with his second. A possible four. Bond took his seven, laid off plenty for the breeze and fired the ball off into the sky. At first he thought he had laid off too much, but then the ball began to float to the left. It pitched and stopped dead in the soft sand blown on to the green from the right-hand bunker. A nasty fifteen-foot putt. Bond would now be glad to get a half. Sure enough Goldfinger putted up to within a yard. That, thought Bond as he squared up to his putt, he will have to hole. He hit his own putt fairly smartly to get it going through the powdering of sand and was horrified to see it going like lightning across the skiddy green. God, he was going to have not a yard, but a two-yard putt back! But suddenly, as if drawn by a magnet, the ball swerved straight for the hole, hit the back of the tin, bounced up and fell in the cup with an audible rattle. The sign from Heaven! Bond went up to Hawker, winked at him and took his driver.

They left the caddies and walked down the slope and back to the next tee. Goldfinger said coldly, "That putt ought to have run off the green."

Bond said off-handedly, "Always give the hole a chance!" He teed up his ball and hit his best drive of the day down the breeze. Wedge and one putt? Goldfinger hit his regulation shot and they walked on again. Bond said, "By the way, what happened to that nice Miss Masterton?"

Goldfinger looked straight in front of him. "She left my employ."

Bond thought, good for her! He said, "Oh, I must get in touch with her again. Where did she go to?"

"I couldn't say." Goldfinger walked away from Bond towards his ball. Bond's drive was out of sight, over the ridge that bisected the fairway. It wouldn't be more than fifty yards from the pin. Bond thought he knew what would be in Goldfinger's mind, what is in most golfers' minds when they smell the first scent of a good lead melting away. Bond wouldn't be surprised to see that grooved swing quicken a trifle. It did. Goldfinger hooked into a bunker on the left of the green.

Now was the moment when it would be the end of the game if Bond made a mistake, let his man off the hook. He had a slight downhill lie, otherwise an easy chip – but to the trickiest green on the course. Bond played it like a man. The ball ended six feet from the pin. Goldfinger played well out of his bunker, but missed the longish putt. Now Bond was only one down.

They halved the dog-leg twelfth in inglorious fives and the longish thirteenth also in fives, Goldfinger having to hole a good putt to do so.

Now a tiny cleft of concentration had appeared on Goldfinger's massive, unlined forehead. He took a drink of water from the tap beside the fourteenth tee. Bond waited for him. He didn't want a sharp clang from that tin cup when it was out-of-bounds over the fence to the right and the drive into the breeze favouring a slice! Bond brought his left hand over to increase his draw and slowed down his swing. The drive, well to the left, was only just adequate, but at least it had stayed in bounds. Goldfinger, apparently unmoved by the out-of-bounds hazard, hit his standard shot. They both negotiated the transverse canal without damage and it was another half in five. Still one down and now only four to play.

The four hundred and sixty yards fifteenth is perhaps the only hole where the long hitter may hope to gain one clear shot. Two smashing woods will just get you over the line of bunkers that lie right up against the green. Goldfinger had to play short of them with his second. He could hardly improve on a five and it was up to Bond to hit a really godlike second shot from a barely adequate drive.

The sun was on its way down and the shadows of the four men were beginning to lengthen. Bond had taken up his stance. It was a good lie. He had kept his driver. There was dead silence as he gave his two incisive waggles. This was going to be a vital stroke. Remember to pause at the top of the swing, come down slow and whip the club head through at the last second. Bond began to take the club back. Something moved at the corner of his right eye. From nowhere the shadow of Goldfinger's huge head approached the ball on the ground, engulfed it and moved on. Bond let his swing take itself to pieces in sections. Then he stood away from his ball and looked up. Goldfinger's feet were still moving. He was looking carefully up at the sky.

"Shades please, Goldfinger." Bond's voice was furiously controlled.

Goldfinger stopped and looked slowly at Bond. The eyebrows were raised a fraction in inquiry. He moved back and stood still, saying nothing.

Bond went back to his ball. Now then, relax! To hell with Goldfinger. Slam that ball on to the green. Just stand still and hit it. There was a moment when the world stood still, then . . . then somehow Bond did hit it – on a low trajectory that mounted gracefully to carry the distant surf of the bunkers. The ball hit the bank below the green, bounced high with the impact and rolled out of sight into the saucer round the pin.

Hawker came up and took the driver out of Bond's hand. They walked on together. Hawker said seriously, "That's one of the finest shots I've seen in thirty years." He lowered his voice. "I thought he'd fixed you then, sir."

"He damned near did, Hawker. It was Alfred Blacking that hit the ball, not me." Bond took out his cigarettes, gave one to Hawker and lit his own. He said quietly, "All square and three to play. We've got to watch those next three holes. Know what I mean?"

"Don't you worry, sir. I'll keep my eye on him."

They came up with the green. Goldfinger had pitched on and had a long putt for a four, but Bond's ball was only just two inches from the hole. Goldfinger picked up his ball and walked off the green. They halved the short sixteenth in good threes. Now there were the two long holes home. Fours would win them. Bond hit a fine drive down the centre. Goldfinger pushed his far out to the right into deep rough. Bond walked along trying not to be too jubilant, trying not to count his chickens. A win for him at this hole and he would need only a half at the eighteenth for the match. He prayed that Goldfinger's ball would be unplayable or, better still, lost.

Hawker had gone on ahead. He had already laid down his bag and was busily – far too busily to Bond's way of thinking – searching for Goldfinger's ball when they came up.

It was bad stuff – jungle country, deep thick luxuriant grass whose roots still held last night's dew. Unless they were very lucky, they couldn't hope to find the ball. After a few minutes' search Goldfinger and his caddie drifted away still wider to where the rough thinned out into isolated tufts. That's good, thought Bond. That wasn't anything like the line. Suddenly he trod on something. Hell and damnation. Should he stamp on it? He shrugged his shoulders, bent down and gently uncovered the ball so as not to improve the lie. Yes, it was a Dunlop 65. "Here you are," he called grudgingly. "Oh no, sorry. You play with a Number One, don't you?"

"Yes," came back Goldfinger's voice impatiently.

"Well, this is a Number Seven." Bond picked it up and walked over to Goldfinger.

Goldfinger gave the ball a cursory glance. He said, "Not mine," and went on poking among the tufts with the head of his driver.

It was a good ball, unmarked and almost new. Bond put it in his pocket and went back to his search. He glanced at his watch. The statutory five minutes was almost up. Another half-minute and by God he was going to claim the hole. Strict rules of golf, Goldfinger had stipulated. All right my friend, you shall have them!

Goldfinger was casting back towards Bond, diligently prodding and shuffling through the grass.

Bond said, "Nearly time, I'm afraid."

Goldfinger grunted. He started to say something when there came a cry from his caddie. "Here you are, sir. Number One Dunlop."

Bond followed Goldfinger over to where the caddie stood on a small plateau of higher ground. He was pointing down. Bond bent and inspected the ball. Yes, an almost new Dunlop One and in an astonishingly good lie. It was miraculous – more than miraculous. Bond stared hard from Goldfinger to his caddie. "Must have had the hell of a lucky kick," he said mildly.

The caddie shrugged his shoulders. Goldfinger's eyes were calm, untroubled. "So it would seem." He turned to his caddie. "I think we can get a spoon to that one, Foulks."

Bond watched thoughtfully and then turned to watch the shot. It was one of Goldfinger's best. It soared over a far shoulder of rough towards the green. Might just have caught the bunker on the right.

Bond walked on to where Hawker, long blade of grass dangling from his wry lips, was standing on the fairway watching the shot finish. Bond smiled bitterly at him. He said in a controlled voice, "Is my good friend in the bunker, or is the bastard on the green?"

"Green, sir," said Hawker unemotionally.

Bond went up to his ball. Now things had got tough again. Once more he was fighting for a half after having a certain win in his pocket. He glanced towards the pin, gauging the distance. This was a tricky one. He said, "Five or six?"

"The six should do it, sir. Nice firm shot." Hawker handed him the club.

Now then, clear your mind. Keep it slow and deliberate. It's an easy shot. Just punch it so that it's got plenty of zip to get up the bank on to the green. Stand still and head down. Click! The ball, hit with a slightly closed face, went off on just the medium trajectory Bond had wanted. It pitched below the bank. It was perfect! No, damn it. It had hit the bank with its second bounce, stopped dead, hesitated and then rolled back and down again. Hell's bells! Was it Hagen who had said, "You drive for show, but you putt for dough?" Getting dead from below that bank was one of the most difficult putts on the course. Bond reached for his cigarettes and lit one, already preparing his mind for the next crucial shot to save the hole – so long as that bastard Goldfinger didn't hole his from thirty feet!

Hawker walked along by his side. Bond said, "Miracle finding that ball."

"It wasn't his ball, sir." Hawker was stating a fact.

"What do you mean?" Bond's voice was tense.

"Money passed, sir. White, probably a fiver. Foulks must have dropped that ball down his trouser leg."

"Hawker!" Bond stopped in his tracks. He looked round. Goldfinger and his caddie were fifty yards away, walking slowly towards the green. Bond said fiercely, "Do you swear to that? How can you be sure?"

Hawker gave a half-ashamed, lop-sided grin. But there was a crafty belligerence in his eye. "Because his ball was lying under my bag of clubs, sir." When he saw Bond's open-mouthed expression he added apologetically, "Sorry, sir. Had to do it after what he's been doing to you. Wouldn't have mentioned it, but I had to let you know he's fixed you again."

Bond had to laugh. He said admiringly, "Well, you *are* a card, Hawker. So you were going to win the match for me all on your own!" He added bitterly, "But, by God, that man's the flaming limit. I've got to get him. I've simply got to. Now let's think!" They walked slowly on.

Bond's left hand was in his trouser pocket, absent-mindedly fingering the ball he had picked up in the rough. Suddenly the message went to his brain. Got it! He came close to Hawker. He glanced across at the others. Goldfinger had stopped. His back was to Bond and he was taking the putter out of his bag. Bond nudged Hawker. "Here, take this." He slipped the ball into the gnarled hand. Bond said softly, urgently, "Be certain you take the flag. When you pick up the balls from the green, whichever way the hole has gone, give Goldfinger this one. Right?"

Hawker walked stolidly forward. His face was expressionless. "Got it, sir," he said in his normal voice. "Will you take the putter for this one?"

"Yes." Bond walked up to his ball. "Give me a line, would you?"

Hawker walked up on to the green. He stood sideways to the line of the putt and then stalked round to behind the flag and crouched. He got up. "Inch outside the right lip, sir. Firm putt. Flag, sir?"

"No. Leave it in, would you?"

Hawker stood away. Goldfinger was standing by his ball on the right of the green. His caddie had stopped at the bottom of the slope. Bond bent to the putt. Come on, Calamity Jane! This one has got to go dead or I'll put you across my knee. Stand still. Club head straight back on the line and follow through towards the hole. Give it a chance. Now! The ball, hit firmly in the middle of the club, had run up the bank and was on its way to the hole. But too hard, damn it! Hit the stick! Obediently the ball curved in, rapped the stick and bounced back three inches – dead as a doornail!

Bond let out a deep sigh and picked up his discarded cigarette. He looked over at Goldfinger. Now then, you bastard. Sweat that one out. And by God if you hole it! But Goldfinger couldn't afford to try. He stopped two feet short. "All right, all right," said Bond generously. "All square and one to go." It was vital that Hawker should pick up the balls. If he had made Goldfinger hole the short putt it would have been Goldfinger who would have picked the ball out of the hole. Anyway, Bond didn't want Goldfinger to miss that putt. That wasn't part of the plan.

Hawker bent down and picked up the balls. He rolled one towards Bond and handed the other to Goldfinger. They walked off the green, Goldfinger leading as usual. Bond noticed Hawker's hand go to his pocket. Now, so long as Goldfinger didn't notice anything on the tee!

But, with all square and one to go, you don't scrutinize your ball. Your motions are more or less automatic. You are thinking of how to place your drive, of whether to go for the green with the second or play to the apron, of the strength of the wind – of the vital figure four that must somehow be achieved to win or at least to halve.

Considering that Bond could hardly wait for Goldfinger to follow him and hit, just once, that treacherous Dunlop Seven that looked so very like a Number One, Bond's own drive down the four hundred and fifty yard eighteenth was praiseworthy. If he wanted to, he could now reach the green – if he wanted to!

Now Goldfinger was on the tee. Now he had bent down. The ball was on the peg, its lying face turned up at him. But Goldfinger had straightened, had stood back, was taking his two deliberate practice swings. He stepped up to the ball cautiously, deliberately. Stood over it, waggled, focusing the ball minutely. Surely he would see! Surely he would stop and bend down at the last minute to inspect the ball! Would the waggle never end? But now the club head was going back, coming down, the left knee bent correctly in towards the ball, the left arm straight as a ramrod. Crack! The ball sailed off, a beautiful drive, as good as Goldfinger had hit, straight down the fairway.

Bond's heart sang. Got you, you bastard! Got you! Blithely Bond stepped down from the tee and strolled off down the fairway planning the next steps which could now be as eccentric, as fiendish as he wished. Goldfinger was beaten already – hoist with his own petard! Now to roast him, slowly, exquisitely.

Bond had no compunction. Goldfinger had cheated him twice and got away with it. But for his cheats at the Virgin and the seventeenth, not to mention his improved lie at the third and the various times he had tried to put Bond off, Goldfinger would have been beaten by now. If it needed one cheat by Bond to rectify the score-sheet that was only poetic justice. And besides, there was more to this than a game of golf. It was Bond's duty to win. By his reading of Goldfinger he *had* to win. If he was beaten, the score between the two men would have been equalized. If he won the match, as he now had, he would be two up on Goldfinger – an intolerable state of affairs, Bond guessed, to a man who saw himself as all powerful. This man Bond, Goldfinger would say to himself, *has* something. He has qualities I can use. He is a tough adventurer with plenty of tricks up his sleeve. This is the sort of man I need for – for what? Bond didn't know. Perhaps there would be nothing for him. Perhaps his reading of Goldfinger was wrong, but there was certainly no other way of creeping up on the man.

Goldfinger cautiously took out his spoon for the longish second over cross-bunkers to the narrow entrance to the green. He made one more practice swing than usual and then hit exactly the right, controlled shot up to the apron. A certain five, probably a four. Much good it would do him!

Bond, after a great show of taking pains, brought his hands down well ahead of the club and smothered his number three iron so that the topped ball barely scrambled over the cross-bunkers. He then wedged the ball on to the green twenty feet past the pin. He was where he wanted to be – enough of a threat to make Goldfinger savour the sweet smell of victory, enough to make Goldfinger really sweat to get his four.

And now Goldfinger really was sweating. There was a savage grin of concentration and greed as he bent to the long putt up the bank and down to the hole. Not too hard, not too soft. Bond could read every anxious thought that would be running through the man's mind. Goldfinger straightened up again, walked deliberately across the green to behind the flag to verify his line. He walked slowly back beside his line, brushing away – carefully, with the back of his hand – a wisp or two of grass, a speck of top-dressing. He bent again and made one or two practice swings and then stood to the putt, the veins standing out on his temples, the cleft of concentration deep between his eyes.

Goldfinger hit the putt and followed through on the line. It was a beautiful putt that stopped six inches past the pin. Now Goldfinger would be sure that unless Bond sank his difficult twenty-footer, the match was his!

Bond went through a long rigmarole of sizing up his putt. He took his time, letting the suspense gather like a thunder cloud round the long shadows on the livid, fateful green.

"Flag out, please. I'm going to sink this one." Bond charged the words with a deadly certitude, while debating whether to miss the hole to the right or the left or leave it short. He bent to the putt and missed the hole well on the right.

"Missed it, by God!" Bond put bitterness and rage into his voice. He walked over to the hole and picked up the two balls, keeping them in full view.

Goldfinger came up. His face was glistening with triumph. "Well, thanks for the game. Seems I was just too good for you, after all."

"You're a good nine handicap," said Bond with just sufficient sourness. He glanced at the balls in his hand to pick out Goldfinger's and hand it to him. He gave a start of surprise. "Hullo!" He looked sharply at Goldfinger. "You play a Number One Dunlop, don't you?"

"Yes, of course." A sixth sense of disaster wiped the triumph off Goldfinger's face. "What is it? What's the matter?"

"Well," said Bond apologetically. "'Fraid you've been playing with the wrong ball. Here's my Penfold Hearts and this is a Number Seven Dunlop." He handed both balls to Goldfinger. Goldfinger tore them off his palm and examined them feverishly.

Slowly the colour flooded over Goldfinger's face. He stood, his mouth working, looking from the balls to Bond and back to the balls.

Bond said softly, "Too bad we were playing to the rules. Afraid that means you lose that hole. And, of course, the match." Bond's eyes observed Goldfinger impassively.

"But, but . . . "

This was what Bond had been looking forward to – the cup dashed from the lips. He stood and watched, saying nothing.

Rage suddenly burst Goldfinger's usually relaxed face like a bomb. "It was a Dunlop Seven you found in the rough. It was your caddie that gave me this ball. On the seventeenth green. He gave me the wrong ball on purpose, the damned che–"

"Here, steady on," said Bond mildly. "You'll get a slander action on your hands if you aren't careful. Hawker, did you give Mr Goldfinger the wrong ball by mistake or anything?"

"No, sir." Hawker's face was stolid. He said indifferently, "If you want my opinion, sir, the mistake may have been made at the seventeenth when the gentleman found his ball pretty far off the line we'd all marked it on. A Seven looks very much like a One. I'd say that's what happened, sir. It would have been a miracle for the gentleman's ball to have ended up as wide as where it was found."

"Tommy rot!" Goldfinger gave a snort of disgust. He turned angrily on Bond. "You saw that was a Number One my caddie found."

Bond shook his head doubtfully. "I didn't really look closely, I'm afraid. However," Bond's voice became brisk, businesslike, "it's really the job of the player to make certain he's using the right ball, isn't it? I can't see that anyone else can be blamed if you tee the wrong ball up and play three shots with it. Anyway," he started walking off the green, "many thanks for the match. We must have it again one day."

Goldfinger, lit with glory by the setting sun, but with a long black shadow tied to his heels, followed Bond slowly, his eyes fixed thoughtfully on Bond's back.'

IAN FLEMING – FROM *GOLDFINGER*

*(A self-satisfied major takes up golf, in order to impress a lady he wishes to marry – only to find it is not as easy as he thought . . . )*

'The morning of the 8th dawned with a warm flush of saffron, rose, and gold, behind which the faint purple of the night that was gone died into the mists of early morning. The pure, sweet air was delicious as the sparkling vapour that rises from a newly opened bottle of invigorating wine. The incoming tide plashed on the beach with lazy and musical kisses, and a soft, melodious wind was stirring the bending grasses that crowned the sand dunes on the outskirts of the links.

I inhaled the glorious air with the rapture of a warrior who sniffs the battle from afar.

(The literary grace of my esteemed journalistic colleague will be observed in the foregoing lines. "It was a ripping morning" was all I actually said to him. – J.W.W.G.)

Kirkintulloch was waiting for me at the first putting green.

I may say at once that during my entire stay at St Magnus I never quite mastered this man's name. It became confused in my mind with other curious-sounding names of Scotch towns, and I addressed him promiscuously as Tullochgorum, Tillicoutry, Auchtermuchty and the like. To his credit, be it said that after one or two attempts to put me right, he suppressed any claim to normal individuality and adapted himself philosophically to my weakness; answering cheerfully to any name that greeted his surprised but resigned ears.

He was the brawny son of honest fisher folk. Of middle height, but sturdily yet flexibly built. His hands were large and horny; his feet, I have no doubt, the same. At all events his boots were of ample proportions. He had blue eyes, with that alert, steady, and far-seeing gaze that is the birthright of folk born to look out over the sea; sandy hair and moustache, and a ruddy colour that suggested equally sunshine, salt winds and whisky. His natural expression was inclined to be sour, but on occasion this was dissipated by a quite genial smile. His manner and address had the odd deferential familiarity that belongs exclusively to the old-fashioned Scotch peasantry. His face I soon found to be a sort of barometer of my progress, for every time I struck a ball I could see exactly the value of the stroke recorded in the grim lines of his weather-beaten features. In movement he was clumsy, except, indeed, when golfing, for then his body and limbs became possessed of that faultless grace which only proficiency in a given line can impart.

"It's a fine moarn fur goalf," was his greeting.

"So I suppose," said I. "Where do we go?"

"We'll gang ower here," he replied, as, tucking my clubs under his arm, he led me in the direction of a comparatively remote part of the links.

As we went I thought it advisable to let him know that, although not yet a golfer I could hold my own in far higher branches of sport. I told him that I was one of the best-known polo players of the day.

There was a considerable pause, but we tramped steadily on.

"Whaat's polo?" said he, at length.

I gave him a brief description of the game.

"Aweel, ye'll no hae a hoarse to help ye at goalf."

"But don't you see, Tullochgorum – "

"Kirkintulloch, sir."

"Kirkintulloch, that the fact of playing a game on ponies makes it much more difficult?"

"Then whaat fur d'ye hae them?"

"Well, it's the game, that's all."

"M'hm" was his sphinx-like response.

I felt that I had not convinced him.

I next hinted that I was a prominent cricketer, and, as a rule, went in first wicket down when playing for my regiment.

"Ay, it's a fine ploy fur laddies."

"It's a game that can only be properly played by men," I replied with indignant warmth.

"Is't?"

"Yes, is't – I mean it is." He had certain phrases that I often unconsciously and involuntarily repeated, generally with ludicrous effect.

The reader, of course, understands that I was not in any sense guilty of such gross taste as to imitate the man to his own ears. I simply could not help pronouncing certain words as he did.

"Aweel, in goalf ye'll no hae a man to birste the ba' to yer bat; ye'll just hae to play it as it lies."

"But, man alive," I cried, " don't you see that to hit a moving object must be infinitely more difficult than to strike a ball that is stationary?"

"Ye've no bunkers at cricket," he replied, with irrelevant but disconcerting conviction, adding, with an indescribable and prophetic relish, "No, nor yet whins."

I could make no impression on this man, and it worried me.

"I take it," I resumed presently, "than what is mainly of importance in golf is a good eye."

"That's ae thing."

"What's ae thing?"

"Yer e'e. The thing is, can ye keep it on the ba'?"

"Of course I can keep it on the ba' – ball."

"We'll see in a meenit," he answered, and stopped. We had reached a large field enclosed by a wall, and here Kirkintulloch dropped the clubs and proceeded to arrange a little heap of damp sand, on which he eventually poised a golf ball.

"Noo, tak' yer driver. Here," and he handed me a beautifully varnished implement decorated with sunk lead, inlaid bone, and resined cord. "Try a swing" – he said "swung" – "like this," and, standing in position before the ball, he proceeded to wave a club of his own in semicircular sweeps as if defying the world in general and myself in particular, till suddenly and rapidly descending on the ball he struck it with such force and accuracy that it shot out into the faint morning mist and disappeared. It was really a remarkably fine shot. I began to feel quite keen.

"Noo, it's your turn," said he, as he teed a second ball, "but hae a wheen practice at the swung first."

So I began "addressing" an imaginary ball.

We wrestled with the peculiar flourishes that are technically known as "addressing the ball" for some minutes, at the end of which my movements resembled those of a man who, having been given a club, was undecided in his mind as to whether he should keep hold of it or throw it away. I wiggled first in one direction, then in another. I described eights and threes, double circles, triangles, and parallelograms in the air, only to be assailed with –

"Na, na!" from Kirkintulloch.

"See here, dae it like this," he cried; and again he flourished his driver with the easy grace of a lifetime's practice.

"I'll tell you what, Kirkudbright – "

"Kirkintulloch, sir."

"Kirkintulloch, just you let me have a smack at the ball."

"Gang on then, sir. Hae a smack."

I took up position. I got my eye on the ball. I wiggled for all I was worth, I swung a mighty swing, I swooped with terrific force down on the ball and behold, when it was all over, there it was still poised on the tee, insolently unmoved, and Kirkintulloch sniffing in the direction of the sea.

"Ye've missed the globe," was his comment. "An' it's a black disgrace to a gowfer."

I settled to the ball again – and with a running accompaniment from Kirkintulloch of "Keep yer eye on the ba'; up wi' yer right fut; tak' plenty time; dinna swee ower fast" – I let drive a second time, with the result that the ball took a series of trifling hops and skips like a startled hare, and deposited itself in rough ground some thirty yards off, at an angle of forty-five degrees from the line I had anxiously hoped to take.

"Ye topped it, sir," was Kirkintulloch's view of the performance.

"I moved it, anyhow," I muttered moodily.

"Ay, ye did that," was the response; "and ye'll never move that ba' again, fur its' doon a rabbit hole and oot o' sight."

Nevertheless, I went steadily on, ball after ball. They took many and devious routes, and entirely different methods of reaching their destinations. Some leapt into the air with a half-hearted and affrighted purpose; others shot along the ground with strange irregularity of direction and distance; a number went off at right or left angles with the pleasing uncertainty that only a beginner can command; whilst not a few merely trickled off the tee in sickly obedience to my misdirected energy. At length I struck one magnificent shot. The ball soared straight and sure from the club just as Kirkintulloch's had, and I felt for the first time the delicious thrill that tingles through the arms right to the very brain, as the clean-struck ball leaves the driver's head. I looked at Kirkintulloch with a proud and gleaming eye.

"No bad," said he, "but ye'll no do that again in a hurry. It was guy like an accident."

"Look here, Kirkincoutry," I said, nettled at last. "It's your business to encourage me, not to throw cold water; and you ought to know it."

"Ma name's Kirkintulloch," he answered phlegmatically; "but it doesna' maitter." (And this was the last time he corrected my errors to his name.) "An' I can tell ye this, that cauld watter keeps the heed cool at goalf, and praise is a snare and a deloosion." Then with the ghost of a smile he added, "Gang on, ye're daein' fine."

The field was now dotted with some fifteen balls at such alarmingly varied distances and angles from the tee that they formed an irregular semicircle in front of us (one ball had even succeeded in travelling backwards); and as I reflected that my original and sustained purpose had been to strike them all in one particular line, I began to perceive undreamt-of difficulties in this royal and ancient game.

But I struggled on, and Kirkintulloch himself admitted that I showed signs of distinct, if spasmodic, improvement. At seven o'clock the driver was temporarily laid aside, and I was introduced in turn to the brassey, the iron, the cleek, the putter and the niblick, the latter a curious implement not unlike a dentist's reflector of magnified proportions. The brassey much resembled the driver, but the iron opened out quite a new field of practice; and my first attempts with it were rather in the nature of sod-cutting with a spade, varied at intervals by deadly strokes that left deep incisions on the ball.

As the clock of the parish church tolled the hour of 8.30, I returned to the hotel with an enormous appetite and a thoughtful mind.'

ROBERT MARSHALL – FROM *THE HAUNTED MAJOR* (1902)

*(An ageing golf champion prepares to play a rising star on a treacherous Hawaiian course, in this first novel by the celebrated golfer and, later, golf commentator Peter Alliss)*

'It snaked along the edge of the cliff, a twisting lovers' knot of brilliant green, scarred by deep ravines, elegantly highlighted by groves of pine, edged, and in places encroached on, by the vivid green-blue of the sea. A new course, a course to test champions. Towering strategically over it, the spindly towers reserved for television and raw wooden stands erected for the hosts of fans already pouring in to watch the ultimate in golfing confrontations. For here the old king would have one last chance to regain his kingdom from the usurper: Duke Denton, idol of golfing's millions, would be matched head to head with Johnny Cornell, the newest and brightest star, with a supporting cast of the best golfers in the world, and before an audience of millions. And where there's fame, there's money. One shrewd promoter, the legendary enigmatic Sam Ross; a galaxy of business and professional managers, including the biggest of them all, Mike Ryan; a horde of hangers-on, male and female – particularly female, for the groupies could be guaranteed to come out in force: and what was in store was the greatest feast of golf ever provided for its enthusiasts, a battle of champions for the richest prize in the game – two million dollars to the winner and everlasting fame as the first ever accredited world champion.

The venue: Hawaii. And the course itself, beautiful, lethal, heartbreaking. The brutal fifth, three hundred and eighty yards of vicious dogleg round a grove of mature pines; the tenth, another dogleg, five hundred and fifty-two yards of twisting fairway bordered by steep cliffs and a hungry sea; the twelfth, with a punishing green set at a nerve-racking slope; the fifteenth, two hundred and eighty-two yards of carry, straight out over the bay on to an island green, with no margin for error, front or back; and finally the eighteenth, truly a hole to crack the tiring nerve, a thin ribbon of turf with the ocean to the left, a canyon to the right, and a final green guarded by a ravine to the front, deep bunkers behind and to the right, and the ubiquitous ocean to the left, a nightmare in its own right and the culminating gut-wrencher in a wind-swept chamber of golfing torture. Whoever mastered such a course, the man whose nerve could hold under the pressure of playing against such natural hazards – and in such hungry company – for four whole days, would indeed be a champion. Hawaii of the World Championship was no place for the faint-hearted, the ill-equipped mentally and physically, the inflated reputation, the has-been. The stage was set for drama; comedy, tragedy, plain farce, the gods of golf would decide – with a little help from some interested parties.'
PETER ALLISS – FROM *THE DUKE*

# STORIES

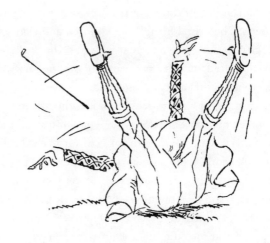

## GOLF FOR DUFFERS
### Sir Henry Rider Haggard

'Oh! well with thee, my brother,
Who hast not known the game,
When early gleams of gladness
Aye set in after sadness;
And still the end is other,
Far other, than the aim.
Oh! well with thee my brother
Who hast not known the game.

So, if memory does not deceive, runs the inspired lay of the bard of the *Saturday Review*. It is of Golf that he sings, not of Nap or Poker, or Pitch-farthing, or any other exciting, but deceitful and deleterious sport. Many have sung and written of it of late, and soon the searcher of bibliographies will find the titles of a multitude of works under the heading "Golf". "What," said a friend to this writer the other day, as he took up Mr Horace Hutchinson's contribution to the Badminton Library, "what, all that great book about hitting a little ball with a stick!" But this and other learned works are written by "golfers of degree", past masters in the art of "hitting the little ball". It yet remains for the subject to be treated from the other side, from the point of view, and for the comfort of, the Duffer. This, the present writer considers himself qualified to do, and for the best of reasons, he wots of none who can play worse than he.

Now as all men know, or ought to know, the game of golf consists in striking a small ball of some hard material into a series of holes – generally eighteen in number – with a variety of wooden and iron-headed clubs, which experience has proved to be the best adapted to the purpose. At first sight this looks easy enough. Indeed, strange as it may seem, the beginner does sometimes find it fairly easy – for the first time or two. He takes the driver with that beautiful confidence which is born of ignorance; hits at the ball somehow, and it goes – somehow; not a full drive of 180 yards or so, indeed, but still a very respectable distance. Arrived safely in the neighbourhood of the first green, he is told that he must putt the ball into a hole about the size of a jam pot. Perhaps he does it at the first attempt, and from a distance whence an experienced player would be quite content to lay his ball near the hole. Then he remarks that "it seems pretty easy". Probably his adversary will assent with a sardonic smile, and wait for the revenge that time will surely bring. He need not wait long; it may be today or tomorrow; but an hour will come when he will see the triumphant tyro scarcely able to hit the ball, much less to send it flying through the air, or wriggling sinuously into the putting-hole, perhaps from a dozen yards away. He will see him cutting up huge lumps of turf behind it – this diversion is called "agriculture" – or smiting it on the head with such force as to drive it into the ground, or "topping" it, so that it rolls meekly into the nearest bush, or "pulling" it into the dyke on the left, or "toeing" it into the sand-bunker on the right; doing everything in short, that he should not do, and leaving undone all those things he should do. For days and weeks he will see him thus employed, and then, if he is a revengeful person, he will take some particularly suitable occasion, when the ball has been totally missed three or four times on the tee, say, to ask, if he, the tyro, "really thinks golf so very easy".

Let none be deceived – as golf is the most delightful game in the world, so it is also the most difficult. It is easier even for a person who has never handled a gun to learn to become a really good shot than for him who has not lifted cleek or driver to bloom into a golfer of the first water. To the young, indeed, all things are possible, but to few of those who begin after thirty will it ever be given to excel. By dint of hard practice and care, in the course of years they may become second- or third-rate players, but for the most part their names will never appear as competitors in the great matches of the world of golf. To begin with, but a small proportion will ever acquire the correct "swing", that is the motion of the arms and club necessary to drive the ball far and sure. We have all heard of and seen the "St Andrews Swing", but how many can practise it with the results common at St Andrews and elsewhere among first-class players? When success attends in the swing, then the ball is topped or heeled, and when the ball goes off well, then the less said about the swing the better. It is instructive to watch any gathering of golfers made up for the most part of players who have not been bred to the game. The majority of them are content with the half-swing, they do not lift the club over the shoulder. If asked their reasons, they will say with truth, that there is only some thirty yards difference between a drive from a half and a drive from a full swing, and that the former is far easier and more certain than the latter. Quite so, but it is not the game; and he who aspires to learn to play the game will prefer to swing full and

fail gloriously rather than to attain a moderate success in this
fashion. But the swing is only one of a hundred arts that have to be
learned before a man can pretend to play golf. Till he has mastered
these, or a goodly proportion of them, he does not play, he only
knocks a ball along, a humble amusement with which alas! most of
us must needs be content for the term of our natural lives. Golf,
like Art, is a goddess whom we must woo from early youth if we
would win her; we must even be born to her worship. No other
skill will avail us here, the most brilliant cricketer does not
necessarily make a first-class golfer; on the contrary, he must begin
by forgetting his cricket; he must not lift himself on his toes and
*hit* like a batsman making a drive. Doubtless, the eye which helps a
man to excel in shooting, at tennis, or cricket, will advantage him
here to some extent, but, on the other hand, he will have much to
forget, much to unlearn. He must clear his mind of all
superstitions, he must humble his pride in the sand, and begin with
a new heart and a meek spirit, well knowing that failure is his goal.
For he will never, never learn to play – it is folly to expect
otherwise. Each evening he will see his mistakes and avow
amendment to himself and to his partner, and yet, when the
morrow is done, will come home murmuring:

> It was last night I swore to thee
> That fond impossibility.

Impossibility! For the middle-aged duffer this word sums it all.

It may be said, Then why have anything to do with such a
hopeless sport? Let him who asks play golf once, and he will
understand why. He will go on playing because he must. Drink,
opium, gambling – from the clutches of all these it is possible to
escape, but from golf, never! Has anybody ever seen a man who
gave up golf? Certainly dead donkeys are more common that these.
Be once beguiled to the investment of five shillings in a driver, and
abandon hope. Your fate is sure. The driver will be broken in a

week, but what will you be? You are doomed for life, or till limbs and eyesight fail you – doomed to strive continually to conquer an unconquerable game. Undoubtedly golf is not so innocent as it seems, it has dangerous possibilities. Can we not easily conceive a man middle-aged, happy, prosperous, regular in his attendance at business, and well satisfied with an annual outing at the seaside? And can we not picture him again after golf has laid its hold upon him? He is no longer happy, for he plays not better and better, but worse and worse. Prosperity has gone, for the time that he should give to work he devotes to the pernicious sport. He has quarrelled with his wife, for has he not broken all the drawing-room china in the course of practising his "swing" on Sundays, and estranged all his friends, who can no longer endure to be bored with his eternal talk of golf? As for the annual outing, it does not satisfy him at all; cost what it will, he needs be on the links five days out of every seven. There is no need to follow him further, or we might dwell on the scene, as yet far off, for this poison is slow, when battered, broken, bankrupt, his very clubs in pawn for a few shillings, he perambulates some third-rate links, no longer as a player, but in the capacity of a superannuated caddie. Here is matter of romance indeed: the motive is generously presented to any novelist weary of portraying the effects of drink and cards. "The Golfer's End; or The Demon Driver", should prove an effective title.

And yet even for those who will never really master it, the game is worth the caddie. To begin with, it has this startling merit, the worse you play the more sport you get. If the fisherman slacks his line, and lets off the salmon, or the shooter misses the only woodcock clean, or the batsman is bowled first ball off a lob, there is an end to those particular delights. But when the golfer tops his ball, or trickles it into a furze-bush, or lands it in a sand-bunker, it is but the beginning of joy, for there it lies patiently awaiting a renewal of his maltreatment. His sport is only limited by the endurance of his muscle, or, perchance, of his clubs, and at the end of the round, whereas the accomplished player will have enjoyed but eighty or a hundred strokes, the duffer can proudly point to a total of twice that number. Moreover he has hurt no one, unless it be the caddie, or the feelings of his partner in a foursome. By the way, the wise duffer should make a point of playing alone, or search out an opponent of equal incapacity; he should not be led into foursomes with members of the golfing aristocracy, that is if he has a proper sense of pride, and a desire not to look ridiculous. He should even avoid the company of members of his own family on these occasions, lest it chance that they lose respect for a man and a father who repeatedly tries to hit a small ball with a stick with the most abject results, and is even betrayed by his failure into the use of language foreign to the domestic hearth. Here is advice for him who has been bitten of this mania. Let him select a little-frequented island links, and practise on them studiously about two hundred days a year for three years or so, either alone, or in the company of others of his own kidney. By this time, unless he is even less gifted than the majority of beginners, he will probably be able to play after a modest and uncertain fashion. Then let him resort to some more fashionable green, and having invested in an entirely new set of clubs, pose before the world as a novice to the game, for thus he will escape the scorn of men. But let him not reverse the process. Thus he who, in his ignorance or pride, takes the train to Wimbledon, and in the presence of forty or fifty masters of the art, solemnly misses the ball three times on the first tee, may perchance never recover from the shock.

Nor will all those years of effort and failure be without their own reward. He will have tramped his gorsey common till every bush and sod is eloquent to him of some past adventure. This is the short green, that by some marvellous accident he once did in *one*, driving his ball from the tee even into the little far-away putting-hole. Here is a spot which he can never pass without a shudder, where he nearly killed his opponent's caddie, that scornful boy who, for many days accustomed to see him topping and putting his ball along from green to green, remained unmoved by his warning shouts of "fore", till one unlucky hour, when by some strange chance he drove full and fair. Crack! went the ball from his brassie. Crack! it came full on the youthful head thirty yards away, and then a yell of agony, and a sickening vision of heels kicking wildly in the air, and presently a sound of clinking silver coin. There, too is the exact place, when for the first (and perchance the last) time he drove over the beetling cliff, and out of the great bunker, the long way too, not the ladies' way – a feat not often accomplished by the skilful. A hundred and ninety-one yards that drive measured, though it is true an envious and long-legged friend who had forced his own ball an inch deep into the sand of the cliff, stepped it at a hundred and eighty-four. He can never forget that supreme moment, it will be with him till his dying hour. Our first large salmon safely brought to bank, a boy's first rocketing pheasant, clean and coolly killed, these afford memories that draw as near to perfect happiness as anything in this imperfect world, but it may be doubted if they can compare to the sense of utter triumph, of ecstatic exhilaration with which, for the first time, we watch the ball, propelled by our unaided skill, soar swiftly out of the horrid depths of an hitherto unconquered bunker. There is a tale – a true one, or it would not be produced here – that, being true, shall be told as an example of noble patience fitly crowned and celebrated.

A wanderer musing in a rugged place was, of a sudden, astonished to see and hear an old gentleman, bearing a curiously shaped stick, walking up and down and chanting the *Nunc Dimittis* as he walked. Moved by curiosity, he came to the aged singer and asked,

"Why do you chant the *Nunc Dimittis* on the edge of this gulf?"

"For this reason, sir," he answered, pointing to the golf-ball that lay upon the turf. "For seventeen years and more I have attempted almost daily to drive a ball across that bunker, and now I have succeeded for the first time. The object of my life is attained, and I am ready to die. That, sir, is why I sing."

Then the wanderer took off his hat, and went away, marvelling at the infatuation of golfers.

It need scarcely be said that the foregoing remarks apply to and are intended for, the consideration of male duffers. It would have been agreeable to extend them to the other sex, but space demands brevity. Golf is a man's game, but here, too women assert their rights. Not that they are all fond of it; by no means. On the contrary, a young lady has been heard, and recently, to express her decided opinion that a law should be passed against its practice during the summer months. This was a lawn-tennis young lady. And another informed this writer that she held golf to be a "horrid game, where everybody goes off like mad, glaring at a little ball, without a word for anybody." Others, it is true, attack the question in a different spirit – they play, and play well. It is curious to observe their style; that they do everything wrong is obvious even to the male incompetent. They stand in front of the ball, they swing their club wildly in preparation, and finally bring it down with an action that suggest reminiscences of a cook jointing veal; but the ball goes, for these young ladies have a good eye and a strong arm. Perhaps no woman player could ever attain to a really first-rate standard, for however vigorous she may be she cannot drive like a man. But with practice there seems to be no reason why she should not approach and putt as well as any man; and certainly she can talk golfing-shop with equal persistency.

And now this duffer will conclude with a word of advice to the world at large – that they should forthwith enter the noble fraternity of duffers, of those who try to play golf and cannot. They will never succeed – at least, not ten per cent of them will succeed. They will knock balls from green to green, and reverence Mr Horace Hutchinson more truly and deeply than the great ones of the earth are generally reverenced; that is all. But they will gain health and strength in the pursuit of a game which has all the advantages of a sport without its expense and cruelty; they will note many a changing light on land and sea; and last, but not least, for several hours a week they will altogether forget their worries, together with Law, Art, Literature or whatever wretched

occupation the Fates have given it to them to follow in the pursuit
of their daily bread. For soon – alas! too soon – the votary of golf
– that great gift of Scotland to the world – will own but one
ambition but rarely to be attained. Thus, he will sing with the poet:

> Who list may grasp at greatness,
> Who list may woo and wive;
> Wealth, wisdom, power, position -
> These make not my ambition.
> Nay but I pray for straightness,
> And do desire to drive.
> Who list may grasp at greatness,
> Who list may woo and wive.'

# A WOMAN IS ONLY A WOMAN
P.G. Wodehouse

'On a fine day in the spring, summer or early autumn, there are few spots more delightful than the terrace in front of our Golf Club. It is a vantage-point peculiarly fitted to the man of philosophic mind: for from it may be seen that varied, never-ending pageant, which men call Golf, in a number of its aspects. To your right, on the first tee, stand the cheery optimists who are about to make their opening drive, happily conscious that even a topped shot will trickle a measurable distance down the steep hill. Away in the valley, directly in front of you, is the lake hole, where these same optimists will be converted to pessimism by the wet splash of a new ball. At your side is the ninth green, with its sinuous undulations which have so often wrecked the returning traveller in sight of home. And at various points within your line of vision are the third tee, the sixth tee, and the sinister bunkers about the eighth green – none of them lacking in food for the reflective mind.

It is on this terrace that the Oldest Member sits, watching the younger generation knocking at the divot. His gaze wanders from Jimmy Fothergill's two-hundred-and-twenty yard drive down the hill to the silver drops that flash up in the sun, as young Freddie Woosley's mashie-shot drops weakly into the waters of the lake. Returning, it rests upon Peter Willard, large and tall, and James Todd, small and slender, as they struggle up the fairway of the ninth.

Love (says the Oldest Member) is an emotion which your true golfer should always treat with suspicion. Do not misunderstand me. I am not saying that love is a bad thing, only that it is an unknown quantity. I have known cases where marriage improved a man's game, and other cases where it seemed to put him right off his stroke. There seems to be no fixed rule. But what I do say is that a golfer should be cautious. He should not be led away by the first pretty face. I will tell you a story that illustrates this point. It is the story of those two men who have just got onto the ninth green – Peter Willard and James Todd.

There is about great friendships between man and man (said the Oldest Member) a certain inevitability that can only be compared with the age-old association of ham and eggs. No one can say when it was these two wholesome and palatable foodstuffs first came together, nor what was the mutual magnetism that brought their deathless partnership about. One simply feels that it is one of the things that must be so. Similarly with men. Who can trace to its first beginnings the love of Damon for Pythias, of David for Jonathan, of Swan for Edgar? Who can explain what it was about Crosse that first attracted Blackwell? We simply say "These men are friends," and leave it at that.

In the case of Peter Willard and James Todd, one may hazard the guess that the first link in the chain that bound them together was the fact that they took up golf within a few days of each other, and contrived, as time went on, to develop such equal form at the game that the most expert critics are still baffled in their efforts to decide which is the worse player. I have heard the point argued a hundred times without any conclusion being reached. Supporters of Peter claim that his driving off the tee entitles him to an unchallenged pre-eminence among the world's most hopeless foozlers – only to be discomfited later when the advocates of James, show, by means of diagrams, that no one has ever surpassed their man in absolute incompetence with the spoon. It is one of those problems where debate is futile.

Few things draw two men together more surely than a mutual inability to master golf, coupled with an intense and ever-increasing love of the game. At the end of the first few months, when a series of costly experiments had convinced both Peter and James that there was not a tottering grey-beard nor a toddling infant in the neighbourhood whose downfall they could encompass, the two became inseparable. It was pleasanter, they found, to play together, and go neck and neck round the eighteen holes, than to take on some lissom youngster who could splatter them all over the course with one old ball and a cut-down cleek stolen from his father; or some spavined elder who not only rubbed it into them, but was apt, between strokes, to bore them with personal reminiscences of the Crimean War. So they began to play together early and late. In the small hours before breakfast, long ere the first faint piping of the waking caddie made itself heard from the caddie-shed, they were half-way through their opening round. And at close of day, when bats wheeled against the steely sky and the "pros" had stolen home to rest, you might see them in the deepening dusk, going through the concluding exercises of their final spasm. After dark, they visited each other's houses and read golf books.

If you have gathered from what I have said that Peter Willard and James Todd were fond of golf, I am satisfied. That is the impression I intend to convey. They were real golfers, for real golf is a thing of the spirit, not of mere mechanical excellence of stroke.

It must not be thought, however, that they devoted too much of their time and their thoughts to golf – assuming, indeed, that such a thing is possible. Each was connected with a business in the metropolis; and often, before he left for the links, Peter would go to the trouble and expense of ringing up the office to say he would not be coming in that day; while I myself have heard James – and this not once, but frequently – say, while lunching at the club-house, that he had half a mind to get Gracechurch Street on the 'phone and ask how things were going. They were, in fact, the type of men of whom England is the proudest – the backbone of a great country, toilers in the mart, untired businessmen, keen red-blooded men of affairs. If they played a little golf besides, who shall blame them?

So they went on, day by day, happy and contented. And then Woman came into their lives, like the Serpent in the Links of Eden, and perhaps for the first time they realized they were not one entity – not one single, indivisible Something that was made for topped drives and short putts – but two individuals, in whose breasts Nature had implanted other desires than the simple ambition to do the dog-leg hole on the second nine in under double figures. My friends tell me that, when I am relating a story, my language is inclined at times a little to obscure my meaning; but, if you understand from what I have been saying that James Todd and Peter Willard both fell in love with the same woman – all right, let us carry on. That is precisely what I was driving at.

I have not the pleasure of an intimate acquaintance with Grace Forrester. I have seen her in the distance, watering the flowers in her garden, and on these occasions her stance struck me as graceful. And once, at a picnic, I observed her killing wasps with a tea-spoon, and was impressed by the freedom of the wrist-action of her back-swing. Beyond this, I can say little. But she must have been attractive, for there can be no doubt of the earnestness with which both Peter and James fell in love with her. I doubt if either slept a wink the night of the dance at which it was their privilege first to meet her.

The next afternoon, happening to encounter Peter in the bunker near the eleventh green, James said:

"That was a nice girl, that Miss What's-her-name."

And Peter, pausing for a moment from his trench-digging, replied:

"Yes."

And then James, with a pang, knew that he had a rival, for he had not mentioned Miss Forrester's name, and yet Peter had divined that it was to her that he had referred.

Love is a fever which, so to speak, drives off without wasting time on the address. On the very next morning after the conversation which I have related, James Todd rang Peter Willard up on the 'phone and cancelled their golf engagements for the day, on the plea of a sprained wrist. Peter, acknowledging the cancellation, stated that he himself had been on the point of ringing James up to say that he would be unable to play owing to a slight headache. They met at tea-time at Miss Forrester's house. James asked how Peter's headache was, and Peter said it was a little better. Peter inquired after James's sprained wrist, and was told it seemed on the mend. Miss Forrester dispensed tea and conversation to both impartially.

They walked home together. After an awkward silence of twenty minutes, James said:

"There is something about the atmosphere – the aura, shall I say? – that emanates from a good woman that makes a man feel that life has a new, a different meaning."

Peter replied:

"Yes."

When they reached James's door, James said:

"I won't ask you in tonight, old man. You want to go home and rest and cure that headache."

"Yes," said Peter.

There was another silence. Peter was thinking that only a couple of days before, James had told him that he had a copy of Sandy MacBean's *How to Become a Scratch Man Your First Season by Studying Photographs* coming by parcel-post from town, and they had arranged to read it aloud together. By now, thought Peter, it must be lying on his friend's table. The thought saddened him. And James, guessing what was in Peter's mind, was saddened too. But he did not waver. He was in no mood to read MacBean's masterpiece that night. In the twenty minutes of silence after leaving Miss Forrester he had realized that "Grace" rhymes with "face", and he wanted to sit alone in his study and write poetry.

The two men parted with a distant nod. I beg your pardon? Yes, you are right. Two distant nods. It was always a failing of mine to count the score erroneously.

It is not my purpose to weary you by a minute recital of the happenings of each day that went by. On the surface, the lives of these two men seemed unchanged. They still played golf together, and during the round achieved towards each other a manner that, superficially, retained all its ancient cheeriness and affection. If – I should say – when, James topped his drive, Peter never failed to say "Hard luck!" And when – or rather if – Peter managed not to top his, James invariably said "Great!" But things were not the same, and they knew it.

It so happened, as it sometimes will on these occasions, for Fate is a dramatist who gets his best effects with a small cast, that Peter Willard and James Todd were the only visible aspirants for the hand of Miss Forrester. Right at the beginning, young Freddie Woosley had seemed attracted by the girl, and had called once or twice with flowers and chocolates, but Freddie's affections never centred themselves on one object for more than a few days, and he had dropped out after the first week. From that time on it became clear to all of us that., if Grace Forrester intended to marry anyone in the place, it would be either James or Peter; and a good deal of interest was taken in the matter by the local sportsmen. So little was known of the form of the two men, neither having figured as a principal in a love-affair before, that even money was the best you could get, and the market was sluggish. I think my own flutter of twelve golf-balls, taken by Percival Brown, was the most substantial of any of the wagers. I selected James as the winner. Why, I can hardly say, unless that he had an aunt who contributed occasional stories to the *Woman's Sphere*. These things sometimes weigh with a girl. On the other hand, George Lucas, who had half-a-dozen of ginger-ale on Peter, based his calculations on the fact that James wore knickerbockers on the links, and that no girl could possibly love a man with calves like that. In short, you see, we had nothing to go on.

Nor had James and Peter. The girl seemed to like them both equally. They never saw her except in each other's company. And it was not until one day when Grace Forrester was knitting a sweater that there seemed a chance of getting a clue to her hidden feelings.

When the news began to spread through the place that Grace was knitting this sweater there was a big sensation. The thing seemed to us practically to amount to a declaration.

That was the view that James Todd and Peter Willard took of it, and they used to call on Grace, watch her knitting and come away with their heads full of complicated calculations. The whole thing hung on one point – to wit, what size the sweater was going to be. If it was large, then is must be for Peter; if small, then James was the lucky man. Neither dared to make open inquiries, but it began to seem almost impossible to find out the truth without them. No masculine eye can reckon up purls and plains and estimate the size of chest which the garment is destined to cover. Moreover, with amateur knitters there must always be allowed a margin for involuntary error. There were many cases during the war where our girls sent sweaters to their sweethearts which would have induced strangulation in their young brothers. The amateur sweater of those days was, in fact, practically tantamount to German propaganda.

Peter and James were accordingly baffled. One evening the sweater would look small, and James would come away jubilant; the next it would have swollen over a vast area, and Peter would walk home singing. The suspense of the two men can readily be imagined. On the one hand, they wanted to know their fate; on the other, they fully realized that whoever the sweater was for would have to wear it. And, as it was a vivid pink and would probably not fit by a mile, their hearts quailed at the prospect.

In all affairs of human tension there must come a breaking point. It came one night as the two men were walking home.

"Peter?" said James, stopping in mid-stride. He mopped his

forehead. His manner had been feverish all the evening.

"Yes?" said Peter.

"I can't stand this any longer. I haven't had a good night's rest for weeks. We must find out definitely which of us is to have that sweater."

"Let's go back and ask her," said Peter.

So they turned back and rang the bell and went into the house and presented themselves before Miss Forrester.

"Lovely evening," said James, to break the ice.

"Superb," said Peter.

"Delightful," said Miss Forrester, looking a little surprised at finding the troupe playing a return date without having booked it in advance.

"To settle a bet," said James, "will you please tell us who – I should say, whom – you are knitting that sweater for?"

"It is not a sweater," replied Miss Forrester, with a womanly candour that well became her. "It is a sock. And it is for my cousin Juliet's youngest son, Willie."

"Good night," said James.

"Good night," said Peter.

"Good night," said Grace Forrester.

It was during the long hours of the night, when ideas so often come to wakeful men, that James was struck by an admirable solution of his and Peter's difficulty. It seemed to him that, were one or the other to leave Woodhaven, the survivor would find himself in a position to conduct his wooing as wooing should be conducted. Hitherto, as I have indicated, neither had allowed the other to be more than a few minutes alone with the girl. They watched each other like hawks. When James called, Peter called. When Peter dropped in, James invariably popped round. The thing had resolved itself into a stalemate.

The idea which now came to James was that he and Peter should settle their rivalry by an eighteen-hole match on the links. He thought very highly of the idea before he finally went to sleep, and

in the morning the scheme looked just as good to him as it had
done overnight.

James was breakfasting next morning, preparatory to going round
to disclose his plan to Peter, when Peter walked in, looking happier
than he had done for days.

"Morning," said James.

"Morning," said Peter.

Peter sat down and toyed absently with a slice of bacon.

"I've got an idea," he said.

"One isn't many," said James bringing his knife down with a jerk-
shot on a fried egg. "What is your idea?"

"Got it last night as I was lying awake. It struck me that, if either
of us was to clear out of this place, the other would have a fair
chance. You know what I mean – with Her. At present we've got
each other stymied. Now, how would it be," said Peter, abstractedly
spreading marmalade on his bacon, "if we were to play an
eighteen-hole match, the loser to leg out of the neighbourhood and
stay away long enough to give the winner the chance to find out
exactly how things stood?"

James started so violently that he struck himself in the left eye with his fork.

"That's exactly the idea I got last night, too."

"Then it's a go?"

"It's the only thing to do."

There was silence for a moment. Both men were thinking. Remember, they were friends. For years they had shared each other's sorrows, joys, and golf-balls, and sliced into the same bunkers.

Presently Peter said:

"I shall miss you."

"What do you mean, miss me?"

"When you're gone. Woodhaven won't seem the same place. But of course you'll be able to come back. I shan't waste any time proposing."

"Leave me your address," said James, "and I'll send you a wire when you can return. You won't be offended if I don't ask you to be best man at the wedding? In the circumstances it might be painful to you."

Peter sighed dreamily.

"We'll have the sitting-room done in blue. Her eyes are blue."

"Remember," said James, "there will always be a knife and fork for you at our little nest. Grace is not the woman to want me to drop my bachelor friends."

"Touching this match," said Peter. "Strict Royal and Ancient rules, of course?"

"Certainly."

"I mean to say – no offence, old man – but no grounding niblicks in bunkers."

"Precisely. And, without hinting at anything personal, the ball shall be considered holed-out only when it is in the hole, not when it stops on the edge."

"Undoubtedly. And – you'll forgive me if I mention it – a player whose ball has fallen in the rough may not pull up all the bushes within a radius of three feet."

"In fact, strict rules."

"Strict rules."

They shook hands without more words. And presently Peter walked out, and James, with a guilty look over his shoulder, took down Sandy MacBean's great work from the bookshelf and began to study the photograph of the short approach-shot showing Mr MacBean swinging from Point A, through dotted line B-C, to Point D, his head remaining the while rigid at the spot marked with a cross. He felt a little guiltily that he had stolen a march on his friend, and that the contest was as good as over.

I cannot recall a lovelier summer day than that on which the great Todd-Willard eighteen-hole match took place. It had rained during the night, and now the sun shone down from a clear blue sky on to turf that glistened more greenly than the young grass of early spring. Butterflies flitted to and fro; birds sang merrily. In short, all Nature smiled. And it is to be doubted if Nature ever had a better cause for smiling – or even laughing outright; for matches like that between James Todd and Peter Willard do not occur every day.

Whether it was that love had keyed them up, or whether hours of study of Braid's *Advanced Golf* and the Badminton Book had produced a belated effect, I cannot say; but both started off quite reasonably well. Our first hole, as you can see, is a bogey four, and James was dead on the pin in seven, leaving Peter, who had twice hit the United Kingdom with his mashie in mistake for the ball, a difficult putt for the half. Only one thing could happen when you left Peter a difficult putt; and James advanced to the lake hole one up, Peter, as he followed, trying to console himself with the thought that many of the best golfers prefer to lose the first hole and save themselves for a strong finish.

Peter and James had played over the lake hole so often that they had become accustomed to it, and had grown into the habit of sinking a ball or two as a preliminary formality with much the

same stoicism displayed by those kings in ancient and
superstitious times who used to fling jewellery into the sea to
propitiate it before they took a voyage. But today, by one of those
miracles without which golf would not be golf, each of them got
over with his first shot – and not only over, but dead on the pin.
Our "pro" himself could not have done better.

I think it was at that point that the two men began to go to
pieces. They were in an excited frame of mind, and this thing
unmanned them. You will no doubt recall Keats's poem about
stout Cortez staring with eagle eyes at the Pacific while all his men
gazed at each other with a wild surmise, silent upon a peak in
Darien. Precisely so did Peter Willard and James Todd stare with
eagle eyes at the second lake hole, and gaze at each other with a
wild surmise, silent upon a tee in Woodhaven. They had dreamed
of such a happening so often and woke to find the vision false,
that at first they could not believe that the thing had actually

occurred.

"I got over!" whispered James, in an awed voice.

"So did I!" muttered Peter.

"In one!"

"With my very first!"

They walked in silence round the edge of the lake, and holed out. One putt was enough for each, and they halved the hole with a two. Peter's previous record was eight, and James had once done a seven. There are times when strong men lose their self-control, and this was one of them. They reached the third tee in a daze, and it was here that mortification began to set in.

The third hole is another bogey four, up the hill and past the tree that serves as a direction-post, the hole itself being out of sight. On his day, James had often done it in ten and Peter in nine; but now they were unnerved. James, who had the honour, shook visibly as he addressed his ball. Three times he swung and only connected with the ozone; the fourth time he topped badly. The discs had been set back a little way, and James had the mournful distinction of breaking a record for the course by playing his fifth shot from the tee. It was a low, raking brassey-shot, which carried a heap of stones twenty feet to the right and finished in a furrow. Peter, meanwhile, had popped up a lofty ball which came to rest behind a stone.

It was now that the rigid rules governing this contest began to take their toll. Had they been playing an ordinary friendly round, each would have teed up on some convenient hillock and probably been past the tree with their second, for James would, in ordinary circumstances, have taken his drive back and regarded the strokes he had made as a little preliminary practice to get him into mid-season form. But today it was war to the niblick, and neither man asked nor expected quarter. Peter's seventh shot dislodged the stone, leaving him a clear field, and James, with his eleventh, extricated himself from the furrow. Fifty feet from the tree James was eighteen, Peter twelve; but then the latter, as every

golfer does at times, suddenly went right off his game. He hit the
tree four times, then hooked into the sand-bunkers to the left of
the hole. James, who had been playing a game that was steady
without being brilliant, was on the green in twenty-six, Peter
taking twenty-seven. Poor putting lost James the hole. Peter was
down in thirty-three, but the pace was too hot for James. He
missed a two-foot putt for the half, and they went to the fourth
tee all square.

The fourth hole follows the curve of the road, on the other side
of which are picturesque woods. It presents no difficulties to the
expert, but it has pitfalls for the novice. The dashing player stands
for a slice, while the more cautious are satisfied if they can clear
the bunker that spans the fairway and lay their ball well out to the
left, whence an iron shot will take them to the green. Peter and
James combined the two policies. Peter aimed to the left and got a
slice, and James, also aiming to the left, topped into the bunker.
Peter, realizing from experience the futility of searching for his
ball in the woods, drove a second, which also disappeared into the
jungle, as did his third. By the time he had joined James in the
bunker he had played his sixth.

It is the glorious uncertainty of golf that makes it the game it is.
The fact that James and Peter, lying side by side in the same
bunker, had played respectively one and six shots, might have
induced an unthinking observer to fancy the chances of the
former. And no doubt, had he not taken seven strokes to extricate
himself from the pit, while his opponent, by some act of God,
contrived to get out in two, James's chances might have been
extremely rosy. As it was, the two men staggered out on to the
fairway again with a score of eight apiece. Once past the bunker
and round the bend of the road, the hole becomes simple. A
judicious use of the cleek put Peter on the green in fourteen,
while James with a Braid iron, reached it in twelve. Peter was
down in seventeen, and James contrived to halve. It was only as he
was leaving the hole that the latter discovered that he had been

putting with his niblick, which cannot have failed to exercise a prejudicial effect on his game. These little incidents are bound to happen when one is in a nervous and highly-strung condition.

The fifth and sixth holes produced no unusual features. Peter won the fifth in eleven, and James the sixth in ten. The short seventh they halved in nine. The eighth, always a tricky hole, they took no liberties with, James, sinking a long putt with his twenty-third, just managing to halve. A ding-dong race up the hill for the ninth found James first at the pin, and they finished the first nine with James one up.

As they left the green James looked a little furtively at his companion.

"You might be strolling on to the tenth," he said. "I want to get a few balls at the shop. And my mashie wants fixing up. I shan't be long."

"I'll come with you," said Peter.

"Don't bother," said James. "You go on and hold our place at the tee."

I regret to say that James was lying. His mashie was in excellent
repair, and he still had a dozen balls in his bag, it being his prudent
practice always to start out with eighteen. No! What he had said
was mere subterfuge. He wanted to go to his locker and snatch a
few minutes with Sandy MacBean's *How to Become a Scratch Man.*
He felt sure that one more glance at the photograph of MacBean
driving would give him the mastery of ths stroke and so enable
him to win the match. In this I think he was a little sanguine. The
difficulty about Sandy MacBean's method of tuition was that he
laid great stress on the fact that the ball should be directly in line
with a point exactly in the centre of the back of the player's neck;
and so far James's efforts to keep his eye on the ball and on the
back of his neck simultaneously had produced no satisfactory
results.

It seemed to James, when he joined Peter on the tenth tee, that
the latter's manner was strange. He was pale. There was a curious
look in his eye.

"James, old man," he said.

"Yes?" said James.

"While you were away I have been thinking. James, old man, do
you really love this girl?"

James stared. A spasm of pain twisted Peter's face.

"Suppose," he said in a low voice, "she were not all you – we –
think she is!"

"What do you mean?"

"Nothing, nothing."

"Miss Forrester is an angel."

"Yes, yes. Quite so."

"I know what it is," said James passionately. "You're trying to
put me off my stroke. You know that the least thing makes me lose
my form."

"No, no!"

"You hope that you can take my mind off the game and make me
go to pieces, and then you'll win the match."

"On the contrary," said Peter. "I intend to forfeit the match."

James reeled.

"What!"

"I give up."

"But – but – " James shook with emotion. His voice quavered.

"Ah!" he cried. "I see now: I understand! You are doing this for me because I am your pal. Peter, this is noble! This is the sort of thing you read about in books. I've seen it in the movies. But I can't accept the sacrifice."

"You must!"

"No, no!"

"I insist!"

"Do you mean this?"

"I give her up, James, old man. I – I hope you will be happy."

"But I don't know what to say. How can I thank you?"

"Don't thank me."

"But, Peter, do you fully realize what you are doing? True, I am one up but there are nine holes to go, and I am not right on my game today. You might easily beat me. Have you forgotten that I once took forty-seven at the dog-leg hole? This may be one of my bad days. Do you understand that if you insist on giving up I shall go to Miss Forrester tonight and propose to her?"

"I understand."

"And yet you stick to it that you are through?"

"I do. And, by the way, there's no need for you to wait till tonight. I saw Miss Forrester just now outside the tennis court. She's alone."

James turned crimson.

"Then I think perhaps –"

"You'd better go to her at once."

"I will." James extended his hand. "Peter, old man, I shall never forget this."

"That's all right."

"What are you going to do?"

"Now, do you mean? Oh, I shall potter round the second nine. If you want me, you'll find me somewhere about."

"You'll come to the wedding, Peter?" said James wistfully.

"Of course," said Peter. "Good luck."

He spoke cheerily, but, when the other had turned to go, he stood looking after him thoughtfully. Then he sighed a heavy sigh.

James approached Miss Forrester with a beating heart. She made a charming picture as she stood there in the sunlight, one hand on her hip, the other swaying a tennis racket.

"How do you do?" said James.

"How are you, Mr Todd? Have you been playing golf?"

"Yes."

"With Mr Willard?"

"Yes. We were having a match."

"Golf," said Grace Forrester, "seems to make men very rude. Mr Willard left me without a word in the middle of our conversation."

James was astonished.

"Were you talking to Peter?"

"Yes. Just now. I can't understand what was the matter with him. He just turned on his heel and swung off."

"You oughtn't to turn on your heel when you swing," said James; "only on the ball of the foot."

"I beg your pardon?"

"Nothing, nothing. I wasn't thinking. The fact is, I've something on my mind. So has Peter. You mustn't think too hardly of him. We have been playing an important match, and it must have got on his nerves. You didn't happen by any chance to be watching us?"

"No."

"Ah! I wish you had seen me at the lake-hole. I did it one under par."

"Was your father playing?"

"You don't understand. I mean I did it one better than even the finest player is supposed to do it. It's a mashie-shot, you know. You mustn't play too light, or you'll fall in the lake; and you mustn't play it too hard, or you go past the hole into the woods. It requires the nicest delicacy and judgement, such as I gave it. You might have to wait a year before seeing anyone do it in two again. I doubt if the "pro" often does it in two. Now, directly we came to this hole today, I made up my mind that there was going to be no mistake. The great secret of any shot is ease, elegance, and the ability to relax. The majority of men, you will find, think it important that their address should be good."

"How snobbish! What does it matter where a man lives?"

"You don't absolutely follow me. I refer to the waggle and the stance before you make the stroke. Most players seem to fix in their minds the appearance of the angles which are presented by the position of the arms, legs and club shaft, and it is largely the desire to retain these angles which results in their moving their heads and stiffening their muscles so that there is no freedom in the swing. There is only one point which vitally affects the stroke, and the only reason why that should be kept constant is that you are enabled to see your ball clearly. That is the pivotal point marked at the base of the neck, and a line drawn from this point to the ball should be at right angles to the line of flight."

James paused for a moment of air, and as he paused, Miss Forrester spoke.

"This is all gibberish to me," she said.

"Gibberish!" gasped James. "I am quoting verbatim from one of the best authorities on golf."

Miss Forrester swung her tennis racket irritably.

"Golf," she said, "bores me pallid. I think it is the silliest game ever invented!"

The trouble about telling a story is that words are so feeble a means of depicting the supreme moments of life. That is where the artist has the supreme advantage over the historian. Were I an

artist, I should show James at this point falling over backwards
with his feet together and his eyes shut, with a semi-circular dotted
line marking the progress of his flight and a few stars above his
head to indicate moral collapse. There are no words that can
adequately describe the sheer, black horror that froze the blood in
his veins as this frightful speech smote his ears.

He had never inquired into Miss Forrester's religious views
before, but he had always assumed that they were sound. And now
here she was polluting the golden summer air with the most
hideous blasphemy. It would be incorrect to say that James's love
was turned to hate. He did not hate Grace. The repulsion he felt
was deeper than mere hate. What he felt was not altogether
loathing and not wholly pity. It was a blend of the two.

There was a tense silence. The listening world stood still. Then,
without a word, James Todd turned and tottered away.

Peter was working moodily in the twelfth bunker when his friend arrived. He looked up with a start. Then, seeing that the other was alone, he came forward hesitatingly.

"Am I to congratulate you?"

James breathed a deep breath.

"On an escape!"

"She refused you?"

"She didn't get the chance. Old man, have you ever sent one right up to the edge of that bunker in front of the seventh and just not gone in?"

"Very rarely."

"I did once. It was my second shot, from a good lie, with the light iron, and I followed well through and thought I had gone just too far, and, when I walked up, there was my ball on the edge of the bunker, nicely teed up on a chunk of grass, so that I was able to lay it dead with my mashie-niblick, holing out in six. Well, what I mean to say is, I feel now as I felt then – as if some unseen power had withheld me in time from some frightful disaster."

"I know just how you feel," said Peter gravely.

"Peter, old man, that girl said golf bored her pallid. She said she thought it was the silliest game ever invented." He paused to mark the effect of his words. Peter merely smiled a faint, wan smile.

"You don't seem revolted," said James.

"I am revolted, but not surprised. You see, she said the same thing to me only a few minutes before."

"She did!"

"It amounted to the same thing. I had just been telling her how I did the lake-hole in two, and she said that in her opinion golf was a game for children with water on the brain who weren't athletic enough to play Animal Grab."

The two men shivered in sympathy.

"There must be insanity in the family," said James at last.

"That," said Peter, "is the charitable explanation."

"We were fortunate to find out in time."

"We were!"

"We mustn't run a risk like that again."

"Never again!"

"I think we had better take up golf really seriously. It will keep us out of mischief."

"You're quite right. We ought to do four rounds a day regularly."

"In spring, summer and autumn. And in winter it would be rash not to practise most of the day at one of those indoor schools."

"We ought to be safe that way."

"Peter, old man," said James, "I've been meaning to speak to you about it for some time. I've got Sandy MacBean's new book, and I think you ought to read it. It is full of helpful hints."

"James!"

"Peter!"

Silently the two men clasped hands. James Todd and Peter Willard were themselves again.

And so (said the Oldest Member) we come back to our original starting-point – to wit, that, while there is nothing definitely to be said against love, your golfer should be extremely careful how he indulges in it. It may improve his game or it may not. But if he finds that there is any danger that it may not – if the object of his affections is not the kind of girl who will listen to him with cheerful sympathy through the long evenings, while he tells her, illustrating stance and grip and swing with the kitchen poker, each detail of the day's round – then, I say unhesitatingly, he had better leave it alone. Love has had a lot of press-agenting from the oldest times; but there are higher, nobler things than love. A woman is only a woman, but a hefty drive is a slosh.'

# A ONE-BALL MATCH
Gerald Batchelor

'It was the first day of Spring and I arrived early on the links, eager to make the most of my holiday.

I found a solitary figure in the smoking-room, poring over the latest book on golf, and recognized him as a fellow member whom I knew to be a good golfer, a good sportsman and one of the pleasantest men in the Club.

Clerkson had retired early from Government service owing to ill-health, and it was understood that, in spite of being an unmarried man, he possessed hardly sufficient means to be able to afford the luxury of playing golf regularly.

"Hullo, Clerkson!" I said, "I haven't seen you here for ages. Have you been away?"

"No," he replied "I – er – I've given up golf."

"Given up golf?" I repeated in amazement, "*you*, the keenest player in all – but you've been ill, perhaps?"

"Yes, I have," he said, "but that is not the real reason. The fact is, I found the game too expensive. I don't complain of my limited income – it is nobody's business but my own – but I don't mind telling you that many a time when I have played here and lost a ball I have been forced to economize by going without my lunch!

"Now you will understand why I have always been so anxious to avail myself of the full five minutes allowed for search, however hopeless the case might appear. It's my own fault for ever taking up golf. I wish I hadn't. No, I don't wish that, and I would willingly deny myself anything rather than be compelled to give it up.

"The limit came when they put up the price of balls. That extra sixpence meant everything to me, you see, so I had no choice but to depart from my earthly paradise.

"I thought I could do it, too, but I was wrong. The exercise of brain and muscle, so happily combined, had become as necessary to me as food and sleep.

"My health began to suffer. Doctors could do nothing. They failed to diagnose my case. I got worse and worse, until I was almost given up.

"This morning I took the matter out of their hands, for I have thought of a plan. I jumped out of bed, enjoyed a big breakfast, and hurried up to the links. I feel better already."

"Excellent!" I exclaimed, "will you have a match?"

"I should be ashamed to ask you to play with me," he replied, "for I'm afraid I might spoil your game."

"What do you mean?" I asked. "You are a better golfer than I am."

"Ah, but I fear you do not quite understand the conditions under which I am compelled to play," he said; "in future I shall always have to play *without a ball!*"

"Without a ball?" I repeated; "you are surely joking. How is it possible?"

"Well, if you really don't object to watching the experiment," said Clerkson, "I will show you."

"Perhaps you will remember," he continued as we made for the first tee, "that it is my custom to take a trial swing before every drive? It was this which suggested the idea. I was always able to judge fairly accurately by the feeling of the swing whether the stroke would have been successful. Will you take the honour?"

"Shall we have a ball on?" I asked as usual, forgetting for the moment the peculiar conditions of the coming match. Clerkson seemed to be engaged in a mental struggle. Then he answered, "Yes!"

I made a fair drive and stood aside to see what my opponent would do. He took some sand, pinched it into a tee, addressed it carefully, and played.

"Ah!" he exclaimed: "I was afraid I should slice. I must have been standing that way."

He made off towards the rough, where I saw him play two strokes, and we walked on together to my ball. I also played two more shots before reaching the green.

"Where are you?" I asked.

"Didn't you see it?" said Clerkson. "I was rather surprised that you did not compliment me on the stroke. It was a wicked lie."

"Are you – are you near the hole?" I inquired, as I settled down to a long putt.

"I don't see it at present," he replied, looking about, "I hope it hasn't run over. Good Heavens!" he went on, as he reached the pin. "It's *in the hole!*"

He stooped and seemed to pick it out.

"I really must apologize for that fluke," my opponent said, as we walked to the next tee, "but I knew it was a fine shot directly I had played it, and I thought it deserved to be pretty close."

"It looks as if this is going to be rather a one-sided match," I said to myself, as I watched him dispatch what he described as a "screamer", and I began to wonder whether Clerkson had planned this game in order to provide himself with the necessary ball.

Knowing him to be a thoroughly good fellow however, I dismissed the suspicion from my mind.

These misgivings prevented me from concentrating my attention entirely on the game, with the result that I played very indifferently and reached the second green three strokes to the bad. After I had holed my putt, Clerkson kept walking up and down the green in his attempts to get into the hole.

"Your hole!" he cried at last; "putting was always my weak point."

The game continued to be very even. If I obtained a lead of one hole my opponent invariably seemed to hit a tremendous distance from the next tee. At the fourth he played a shot which must have easily beaten the record drive. On the other hand, if he happened to become one up he lost the next by taking three or four putts.

At the sixth hole his ball disappeared into a gorse bush. Formerly he would have been much disturbed by such an occurrence, but now he seemed to accept the situation with philosophic calm.

"Come along; never mind," he said, after a casual look round; "it's of no consequence; only an old gutta, you know. I'll drop another" – which he did. He must have lost quite half a dozen balls during the round.

At the ninth we were all square. I was beginning to find my game better now.

"Mark it!" cried Clerkson, directly after driving from the tenth tee; "I've lost it in the sun."

"I see it," I said; "you've pulled it rather badly, I'm afraid, and it has landed in 'Purgatory' bunker." I pointed out to him that it was lying in a hopeless position, and he gave up the hole.

At the twelfth hole Clerkson made a very serious error of judgement. I was diligently looking for his wild drive when I happened to stumble on a brand-new "Dunlop".

"What are you playing with?" I asked.

"Let me see," he said, watching my face very intently, "was it a

'Colonel', or a 'Zodiac', or a 'Silver King', or – oh, I know; it was a 'Challenger'."

I put the ball in my pocket.

At the fourteenth, where Clerkson had the honour, some workmen were walking across the fairway, quite three hundred yards away.

"Do you think I can reach them?" my opponent said. I thoughtlessly said, "No, of course not."

Directly he had driven he yelled "Fore!" at the top of his voice. The men looked round.

"That was a narrow escape," he gasped.

"But surely you were a long way short," I said.

"Short!" he exclaimed, "why, man, it was *right over their heads!*"

He gave me a rare fright at the next.

I had a splendid tee shot, for once, and Clerkson walked straight up to my ball.

"This is mine, I believe," he said.

"Certainly not," I cried, "I am playing with a 'Kite'."

"*So am I!*" said he.

Fortunately I was able to point out a private mark which I had made on my ball.

We were all square on the eighteenth. I drove out of bounds.

"Did you get a good one?" I asked anxiously, after he had played.

"A perfect peach," he replied.

I concluded that I had lost the match. I persevered, however, and was playing two more with my approach, while he (so I was informed) was less than a yard from the hole. My mashie shot looked like going in, but the ball came to rest on the edge of the tin.

Clerkson walked up, looked at the ball, went on one knee, then suddenly dashed his cap to the ground in disgust.

"Anything wrong?" I inquired.

"Wrong?" he repeated. "Can't you see that you have laid me *a dead stymie?*"

He studied the line with great care.

"I think there is just room to pull round," he muttered.

He played, and watched, with an agonized expression, the course of his invisible ball. Suddenly there came a strong puff of wind, and my ball toppled into the hole.

"D—n it all," cried Clerkson, "I've *knocked you in!*"

He picked up my ball, and with it, apparently, his own.

"A halved match," he said, "and I must thank you for an exceedingly interesting game."

I was due in London that evening, and on my return, some weeks later, I learnt that Clerkson had been laid up with a form of brain fever.'

# THE GOLFOMANIAC
### Stephen Leacock

'We ride in and out pretty often together, he and I, on a suburban train.

That's how I came to talk to him. "Fine morning," I said as I sat down beside him yesterday and opened a newspaper.

"Great!" he answered. "The grass is drying out fast now and the greens will soon be all right to play."

"Yes," I said, "the sun is getting higher and the days are decidedly lengthening."

"For the matter of that," said my friend, "a man could begin to play at six in the morning easily. In fact, I've often wondered that there is little golf played before breakfast. We happened to be talking about golf, a few of us last night – I don't know how it came up – and we were saying that it seems a pity that some of the best part of the day, say, from five o'clock to seven thirty, is never used."

"That's true," I answered, and then, to shift the subject, I said, looking out of the window:

"It's a pretty bit of country just here, isn't it?"

"It is," he replied, "but it seems a shame they make no use of it – just a few market gardens and things like that. Why, I noticed along here acres and acres of just glass – some kind of houses for plants or something – and whole fields of lettuces and things like that. It's a pity they don't make something of it. I was remarking only the other day as I came along in the train with a friend of mine, that you could easily lay out an eighteen-hole course anywhere here."

"Could you?" I said.

"Oh, yes. This ground, you know, is an excellent light soil to shovel up into bunkers. You could drive some ditches through it and make one or two deep holes – the kind they have on some of the French links. In fact, improve it to any extent."

I glanced at my morning paper. "I see," I said, "that it is again rumoured that Lloyd George is at last definitely to retire."

"Funny thing about Lloyd George," answered my friend. "He never played, you know; most extraordinary thing – don't you think? – for a man in his position. Balfour, of course, was very different: I remember when I was over in Scotland last summer I had the honour of going around the course at Dumfries just after Lord Balfour. Pretty interesting experience, don't you think?"

"Were you over on business?" I asked.

"No, not exactly. I went to get a golf ball, a particular golf ball. Of course, I didn't go merely for that. I wanted to get a mashie as well. The only way, you know, to get what you want is to go to Scotland for it."

"Did you see much of Scotland?"

"I saw it all. I was on the links at St Andrew's and I visited the

Loch Lomond course and the course at Inverness. In fact, I saw everything."

"It's an interesting country, isn't it, historically?"

"It certainly is. Do you know they have played there for over five hundred years! Think of it! They showed me at Loch Lomond the place where they said Robert the Bruce played the Red Douglas (I think that was the party – at any rate, Bruce was one of them), and I saw where Bonnie Prince Charlie disguised himself as a caddie when the Duke of Cumberland's soldiers were looking for him. Oh, it's a wonderful country historically."

After that I let a silence intervene so as to get a new start. Then I looked up again from my newspaper.

"Look at this," I said pointing to a headline, *United States Navy Ordered Again to Nicaragua*. "Looks like more trouble, doesn't it?"

"Did you see in the paper a while back," said my companion, "that the United States Navy Department is now making golf compulsory at the training school at Annapolis? That's progressive, isn't it? I suppose it will have to mean shorter cruises at sea; in fact, probably lessen the use of the Navy for sea purposes. But it will raise the standard."

"I suppose so," I answered. "Did you read about this extraordinary murder case in Long Island?"

"No," he said. "I never read murder cases. They don't interest me. In fact, I think the whole continent is getting over-preoccupied with them – "

"Yes, but this case had such odd features –"

"Oh, they all have," he replied, with an air of weariness. "Each one is just boomed by the papers to make it a sensation – "

"I know, but in this case it seems as if the man was killed with a blow from a golf club."

"What's that? Eh, what's that? Killed with a blow from a golf club?"

"Yes, some kind of club – "

"I wonder if it was an iron – let me see the paper – though, for the matter of that I imagine a blow from even a wooden driver, let alone one of the steel-handled drivers – where does it say it? – pshaw, it only just says 'a blow with a golf club'. It's a pity the papers don't write these things up with more detail, isn't it? But perhaps it will be better in the afternoon paper –"

"Have you played golf much?" I inquired. I saw it was no use to talk of anything else.

"No," answered my companion, "I am sorry to say I haven't. You see, I began late. I've only played twenty years, twenty-one if you count the year that's beginning in May. I don't know what I was doing. I wasted about half my life. In fact, it wasn't till I was well over thirty that I caught on to the game. I suppose a lot of us look back over our lives that way and realize what we have lost.

"And even as it is," he continued, "I don't get much chance to play. At the best I can only manage about four afternoons a week, though of course I get most of Saturday and all of Sunday. I get my holiday in the summer, but it's only a month, and that's nothing. In the winter I manage to take a run south for a game once or twice and perhaps a little swack at it around Easter, but only a week at a time. I'm too busy – that's the plain truth of it." He sighed. "It's hard to leave the office before two," he said. "Something always turns up."

And after that he went on to tell me something of the technique of the game, illustrate it with a golf ball on the seat of the car, and the peculiar mental poise needed for driving, and the neat, quick action of the wrist (he showed me how it worked) that is needed to undercut a ball so that it flies straight up in the air. He explained to me how you can do practically anything with a golf ball, provided that you keep your mind absolutely poised and your eye in shape and your body a trained machine. It appears that even Bobby Jones of Atlanta and people like that fall short very often from the high standard set by my friend in the suburban car.

So, later in the day, meeting someone in my club who was a person of authority on such things, I made inquiry about my friend. "I rode into town with Llewellyn Smith," I said. "I think he belongs to your golf club. He's a great player, isn't he?"

"A great player!" laughed the expert. "Llewellyn Smith? Why, he can hardly hit a ball! And anyway, he's only played about twenty years!"'

## AN UNLUCKY GOLFER
A.A. Milne

'I am the world's unluckiest golfer.

Yes, I know what you are going to say, but I don't mean what you mean. Of the ordinary bad luck which comes to us all at times I do not complain. It is the "rub of the green". When my best drive is caught by cover, or fielded smartly by mid-on with his foot; when I elect to run a bunker ten yards away and am most unfortunately held up by blown sand (or, as I generally call it, dashed sand); when I arrive at last on the green, and my only hope of winning the hole is that my opponents shall pick up a worm which he ought to have brushed away, or brush away one which he ought to have picked up . . . and there are no worms out this morning; on all these occasions I take my ill-luck with a shrug of the shoulders and something as nearly like a smile as I can manage. After all, golf would be a very dull game if it were entirely a matter of skill.

It is in another way altogether that I am singled out by Fate. Once I have driven off the first tee, she is no more unkind to me than to the others. By that time she has done her worst. But sometimes it is as much as I can do to get onto the first tee at all, so relentless is her persecution of me. Surely no other golfer is so obstructed.

I suppose my real trouble is that I take golf too seriously. When I arranged many years ago to be at St Margaret's at 2.30 on Wednesday, I *was* at St Margaret's at 2.30 on Wednesday. I didn't ring up suddenly and say that I had a cold, or that my dog wanted a run, or that a set of proofs had just arrived which had to be corrected quickly. No, I told myself that an engagement was an engagement. *"Wednesday, St Margaret's 2.30"* – I turned up, and have never regretted it. If today my appointment is *"Sunningdale, Thursday, 10.45"*, it is as certain that I shall be there. But these other golfers, one wonders how they ever get married at all.

I am not saying that they are careless about their promises; not all of them; but that, in their case, the mere fact of making an important appointment seems to bring out something: spots or a jury-summons or a new baby. I suppose that, when they play with each other, they hardly notice these obstructions, for if A has to plead an unexpected christening on the Monday, B practically knows he has to have his tonsils removed suddenly on the Thursday, when the return match is to be played; wherefore neither feels resentment against the other. "Tonsils, juries, christenings," I say to myself, "but I thought we were playing *golf*."

But not only am I a serious golfer, I am, as I have said, the world's unluckiest one. The most amazing things happen to the people who arrange to play with me. On the very morning of our game they are arrested for murder, summoned to Buckingham Palace, removed to asylums, sent disguised to Tibet, or asked to play the leading part in *Hamlet* at twenty-four hours' notice. Any actor out of work would be wise to fix up a game with me for on that day he would almost certainly be sent for to start rehearsing. Of course he might have a fatal accident instead, but that is a risk which he would have to take.

However, it is time that you saw my golf in action. Here, then, is a typical day, unexaggerated.

On a certain Wednesday I was to play a couple of rounds with a friend. On Tuesday afternoon I rang him up on the telephone to remind him of our engagement, and in the course of a little talk before we hung our receivers up, I said that I had just been lunching with an actor-manager, and he said that he had just been bitten by a mosquito. Not that it mattered to the other in the least, but one must have one's twopennyworth.

Wednesday dawned, as it has a habit of doing, but never did it dawn so beautifully as now; the beginning of one of those lovely days of early autumn than which nothing is more lovely. That I was to spend the whole of this beautiful day playing golf, not working, was almost too good to be believed. I sang as I climbed into my knickerbockers; I was still singing as I arranged the tassels of my garters . . . And, as I went down to breakfast, the telephone began to ring.

I knew at once, of course. With all the experience I have had, I knew. I merely wondered whether it was the man himself who was dead, or one of his friends.

"Hallo!" said his voice. So he was alive.

"Yes?" I said coldly.

"Hallo! I say, you remember the mosquito?" (*Which mosquito?*) "Well, my leg is about three times its ordinary size." (*Does that matter? I thought. None of us is really symmetrical.*) "I can hardly move it . . . Doctors . . . Nurses . . . Amputate . . . In bed for a year . . . " He babbled on, but I was not listening. I was wondering if I could possibly find somebody else. It is a funny thing, but somehow I cannot write in knickerbockers. Once I have put them on, I find it impossible to work. I *must* play golf. But alas! how difficult to find another at such short notice. As a last hope I decided to ring up Z. Z. is almost as keen a golfer as myself. No such trifle as a lack of uniformity in his legs would keep *him* from his game. I cut off the other fellow as he was getting to the middle of his third operation, and got on to Z. Z, thank Heaven for him, would play.

I called for him. We drove down. We arrived. With each succeeding minute, the morning became more lovely; with each succeeding minute I thanked Heaven more for Z. As we walked over to the caddie-master I was almost crying with happiness. Never was there day more beautiful. All this mosquito business had made us late, and there were no caddies left, but did I mind? Not a bit! On a morning like this, I thought to myself as I stepped on to the first tee, I couldn't mind anything.

The moment that Z. stepped on to the first tee, I knew that I was mistaken. You will never believe it, but I give you my word that it is true. Z. stepped on to the wrong bit of the first tee, uttered one loud yell . . . and collapsed on the grass with a broken ankle . . .

You say that I might have left him there and played a few holes by myself? I did. But it was necessary to give instructions for him to be removed before others came after me. I forget the exact rule about loose bodies on the tee, but a fussy player might easily have objected. So I had to go back and tell the secretary, and one way and another I was delayed a good deal. And of course it spoiled my day entirely.

But I was not surprised. As I say, I am the world's unluckiest golfer.'

# RETIRED GOLF
## Harry Graham

I

'It has been roughly estimated by competent statisticians that within comparatively recent times the game of golf has increased the cost of the State pension list by an annual sum of not less than £200,000. Before the Scottish national pastime had attained its present almost universal popularity, it was the fashion for superannuated officials who were past their work to betake themselves to cheerless villas in the neighbourhood of Camberley or Canterbury, where they strove to mitigate the tedium of a miserable existence of enforced leisure by writing violent letters to the newspapers to complain of the decadence of their native land.

Veteran Civil Servants spent the evenings of their lives giving the

dog a run in a suburban lane, or tricycling to the local post-office
to inquire if there were any letters for Pondicherry Lodge or The
Chestnuts. Retired Major-Generals were compelled to simulate a
fictitious interest in intensive gardening or philately; grey-headed
Rear-Admirals of the Blue wasted upon their wives or domestics
that wealth of cosmopolitan invective which they had laboriously
acquired in various parts of the world in the course of a hectic and
successful naval career. Imprecations that had sent a shudder of
apprehension rippling from stem to stern of a British battleship
spent themselves harmlessly upon the hardened ears of devoted
help-meet or female retainer; the rich beauty of a lurid vocabulary
that had been the envy of many a quarter-deck was lost upon the
jobbing gardener, while objurations that had driven able-bodied
seamen to cling in terror to the aft hatchways left the boot-boy
comparatively cold.

Thus, thwarted at every turn, hemmed in by the narrow
boundaries of parochial life, with no outlet for his energies, no
safety-valve for those eccentricities of temper that he had
cultivated so assiduously in every corner of the globe, the retired
official became a prey to those morbid self-analytical thoughts
which, fostered by periodical attacks of gout, and liberally
stimulated with doses of rare old tawny port at two shillings the
bottle, led often enough to a premature and untimely decease.
Major-Generals perished of suppressed passion before they had
reached seventy; Indian Civil Servants acquired the fatal bath-chair
habit while still in their prime; and few pensioners survived for any
length of time to enjoy the £200 or so a year with which a grateful
country rewards those who have devoted the best part of their life
to its service.

This sad state of affairs has been mercifully put to an end by the
discovery of a game which not only prolongs the span of human
existence and reduces the ranks of the chronically moribund, but
also invests the lives of the aged with an interest that
unquestionably enhances their domestic happiness, and renders

many of them quite tolerable husbands and fathers.

The victim of advancing years, of senile decay, of incipient dotage, may find in golf a panacea for, a palliative of, almost every mental and physical disability under which he happens to labour; the martyr to that nervous irritability which too often accompanies second childhood is supplied with a fresh channel for the expression of those thoughts which, if unhealthily restrained, cast their shadow over home-life and bring discord into the family circle.

I knew a retired Army Colonel who at one time used to make his wife's existence a positive burden to her by abusing the cooking; who habitually sat at meals in a gloomy silence that was only broken by the sound of his plate being pushed away from him with a snort of disgust. To-day, since he has taken to golf, this man is an altered being, displaying a healthy appetite for whatever food is placed before him, and talking happily away all through dinner upon the subject in which he is now absorbingly interested. Often, indeed, his flow of genial garrulity continues until long after bedtime; he will keep his wife awake half the night describing the three perfect putts he made upon the last green; he will rouse her at 2 a.m. to tell her of a mashie shot which he had forgotten to mention at dinner, and far into the dawn his voice can be heard explaining to a snoring and unconscious spouse that he would assuredly have done the fourth hole in six if only he hadn't missed his drive, required three strokes to get out of a bunker, and taken four more to hole out.

Again, a Rear-Admiral of my acquaintance, the violence of whose language had long rendered him an insupportable inmate of any respectable household became a reformed character once he had learnt to play golf. After spending a strenuous day hacking his ball from tussock to tussock in the "rough" at Walton Heath, he would return home so hoarse and exhausted as to be unable to utter a single word of reproof to his family. In the Navy he had been justly considered unique as a master of invective, but on the golf-links he often became inspired by adverse fortune to surpass even his own earlier efforts, and the heights of eloquence to which he soared, the maledictory phrases which he spontaneously coined in his attempts to do justice to his outraged feelings, earned him the admiration of local Masters of Hounds, and would have wrung reluctant tributes from the most imaginative fish-porters in Billingsgate.

## II

It is not my purpose in these pages to deal with the technicalities of golf, nor yet to emulate the literary labours of such expert essayists as Braid, Vardon or Taylor. Of what is known as "Advanced Golf" these writers have treated in a manner which less competent masters of English prose may well have cause to envy; they have covered the whole ground so completely that nothing remains to be said upon this particular aspect of the game.

Very little, however, has yet been written upon the subject of what (for lack of a better term) I may venture to call "Retired Golf" – that is to say, golf for the elderly, for players whose handicap ranges between 18 and 36, who may truthfully be said to have one foot in the grave and the other almost continually in some bunker. And it is to these, as well as to the mentally deficient, the morally and physically infirm, and to all natural and incurable foozlers, that I propose to address a few words of counsel and encouragement, in the hope that by so doing I may possibly help to improve their game, and thus add not a little to the sum of human happiness.

The whole secret of success at retired golf, as everybody nowadays admits, lies in the ability of the player to strike the ball *without moving his head*. The constantly repeated injunction to "keep your eye on the ball" is, indeed, very often misleading, this optical immobility being only enjoined as the most practical method of ensuring that the head shall be kept perfectly still.

Few men, alas! are privileged to possess swivel-eyes, and for those fortunate beings who are thus naturally equipped with the advantages usually monopolized by chameleons it is easy to remove the gaze without shifting the head. But with the majority of mankind the eye cannot be raised with impunity, the temptation to lift up their heads – after the fashion of the Psalmist's everlasting gates – at the moment of hitting the ball being almost irresistible. Many systems have therefore been invented by golfers anxious to break themselves of this pernicious habit, but it will be sufficient for my purpose if I describe the two most successful now in vogue at St Andrews.

The first (and perhaps the simplest) consists of wearing a tall hat in which a number of small sleigh-bells have been carefully concealed. It then becomes the player's chief ambition to strike his ball without ringing the bells, and whenever he succeeds in doing so he may be quite sure that, whatever other fault he may have committed, he has not moved his head. That occasionally, even in such circumstances, his strike falls short of perfection may be accounted for by the fact that he has pulled his arms in, pushed his elbows out, shifted his feet, altered his stance, lost his balance, or been guilty or one or other of the thousand minor crimes with which the path of the golfer is beset.

The top-hat method, however, possesses certain inevitable drawbacks, some of which are so patent as scarcely to require mention. I remember once at Sandwich, when I happened to be wearing the sleighbell form of headgear, and was strolling along the fairway in a very musical fashion, a parlourmaid came running out of an adjacent villa, under the impression that I was the local muffin-man, and, pressing sixpence into my unwilling palm, besought me to supply her with half a dozen of my choicest crumpets for her mistress's afternoon tea. Not happening on this particular afternoon to have any crumpets about me, my confusion may well be imagined.

On another occasion, at Brancaster, I was followed for miles along the "pretty" by some two hundred bleating sheep, who had mistaken me for the bell-wether of the flock; and when a couple of short-horn cattle joined the procession, the congestion upon the putting-greens became so great that, at my opponent's urgent request, I consented to doff the offending hat, and bury the sleigh-bells in a bunker.

A much simpler way of keeping the head immovable consists of tying a stout string to a tooth in the lower jaw, passing the end between one's legs, and getting a caddy to hold it tightly behind one's back while one is addressing the ball. In this case any attempt to jerk the head up results in the loss of a favourite molar, and it is safe to assume that a man of even moderate intelligence will gladly renounce the most seductive of bad habits before excessive indulgence therein has left him completely toothless. To prove the efficacy of this system I have but to mention that in the summer of 1907 I succeeded in reducing my handicap from 32 to 28 at the negligible cost of two wisdom teeth. Need I say more?

I cannot honestly recommend the practice in vogue among some of the older habitués of our Lowland golf-courses who paint a large human eye upon their golf-ball, and have it teed up in such a way that it glares upon the player with a passionate intensity which makes it almost impossible for him to look away.

This may be satisfactory enough on the tee, unfortunately, the painted eye will not always remain uppermost when once the ball is in play, and it becomes a difficult matter to negotiate a successful approach shot with a ball that is either gazing invitingly into an impending hazard or seems to be winking sardonically up at one from the "rough".

The late Lord Chorlesbury always used a ball of this kind, and I shall never forget the panic that ensued among the nurses and children who spend their days on the beach to the right of the third tee at North Berwick when what appeared to be a gigantic human (or, as some of them thought, Divine) eye fell in their midst from the blue vault of Heaven above.

Two French governesses, professed atheists, who happened to be bathing in the sea, and were at the same time engaged in a theological discussion in which they ridiculed the alleged immanence of a Supreme Being, were converted then and there to a mild form of agnosticism, and reluctantly admitted the plausibility of that uncomfortable doctrine which presupposes the perpetual presence of a Divine Power "about one's bath, and about one's bed, and spying out all one's ways".

In spite of this system, however, Lord Chorlesbury was probably the most erratic driver in the world. He is the only man I have ever met who could strike his ball so far back on the heel of his club that it would speed through his legs at right angles from the tee, and injure an inoffensive caddy standing behind him. To play as his partner or opponent was to take one's life in one's hand; and it was with especial reference to his peculiar method that the Bishop of Deal composed that well-known hymn "For those in Peril on the Tee", which has since become so popular with mixed foursomes on every seaside course in Christendom.

## III

Once the player has learnt to control the movements of his head he may be said to have mastered the game of golf, and can confidently set forth to give an exhibition of his prowess upon the most crowded links without any very serious internal misgivings. There are, however, one or two minor points of golfing etiquette with which it is as well that he should be acquainted if he desires to be regarded as an attractive partner or a tolerable opponent.

When two second-class players start out together from the club-house to enjoy a friendly match, it is always considered proper for each of them to deprecate his own skill, and express modest doubts as to his own ability to provide his companion with a good game.

"I don't feel as if I should be able to hit the ball at all," he murmurs diffidently. "I haven't played for weeks."

"Nor I," replies his friend. "I expect you'll beat me hollow. I've got a groggy elbow, too."

"I'm sorry to hear that," says the first. "To tell you the truth, I'm not feeling very fit myself. We sat up playing bridge last night till any hour and . . . "

"I never sleep well in this place; I don't know why it is, I'm sure. And with my groggy elbow . . . "

"You ought to give me a stroke a hole, at least . . . "

"My dear chap! What's your handicap?"

"I don't believe I've got one. I play so little. What's yours?"

"Mine? Oh, mine's anything between eighteen and twenty. And then with my groggy elbow . . . "

"How do you and Jones play together?"

"Oh, he beats me easily. At least, last time we played he gave me a half and won, six up; but then I must admit I had the most infernal luck and got into every single bunker on the course. I began right enough; did the first hole in nine, the second in eleven, and the third in eight. After that I seemed to go all to pieces."

"Suppose we play even?"

"Righto! After all, so long as we have decent game, it doesn't matter much who wins."

And at golf, fortunately, a decent game can always be obtained. It is, indeed, one of the chief charms of this attractive pastime that, by means of a system of tactful handicapping, players of every degree and class may be evenly matched against one another in a fashion that can seldom be accomplished at other games. A single bad lawn-tennis player will ruin a whole set; at croquet or billiards the man who is matched against a champion spends most of his time idly watching his opponent playing, and only issues at rare intervals from a retirement into which he is almost immediately driven back. At golf, on the other hand, the receipt of a few strokes enables an indifferent performer to hold his own against a superior adversary, and there are other methods by which golfers of varying skill can be placed upon an equal footing.

It is, of course, notorious that the player who is permitted under the terms of his handicap to shout "Boo!" in the ear of an opponent three times in the course of a round, just as the unfortunate man is addressing his ball, possesses an advantage which should always enable him to secure the match. The right to "Boo!" need never, as a matter of fact, be exercised, the mere knowledge that this exclamation is perpetually dangling like the sword of Damocles over his head being as a rule quite sufficient to put the most experienced player off his game. With eighteen bisques and a couple of "Boos!" I should be quite ready to challenge Vardon himself.

IV

Golf has frequently been labelled a selfish game by persons who do not indulge in the sport; nevertheless, it may be justly affirmed that scarcely a round passes without providing opportunities for a display of generosity, patience, and other kindred virtues, of which unselfishness is the very essence.

It is, for instance, an essential characteristic of the true golfer that he should be able to praise an opponent's good strokes and sympathize with his bad ones in a natural and whole-hearted fashion, and at the shortest possible notice. When he is four down at the turn, and his adversary lays his second shot dead, or when his rival's drive drops like a stone into a bunker, it is no easy task to exclaim "Well played!" or "Bad luck!" (as the case may be) in tones that carry conviction. "In thinking of the sorrows of others," as a great philosopher once remarked, "we forget our own," and the truth of this saying is nowhere more apparent than upon the golf-links.

The perfect golfer should always be ready to listen with a kindly ear to all the reasons his opponent insists upon giving him for missing various easy shots; he should at the same time remember that nobody really cares for unsolicited information of this kind, and should refrain from remarking, after he has foozled a particularly easy mashie-shot: "My ball was lying in a hole!" "I looked up!" or "My caddy gave me the wrong club!"

Long experience upon the links teaches one to be genially tolerant of the mathematical miscalculations of others. It is a strange thing that men who invariably add up a bridge score correctly – City magnates, captains of industry, masters of finance who can tell offhand the profit they have made on 460 Canadian Pacific ordinary shares when the stock rises 3 – often display a lamentable incapacity for estimating the exact number of times they have struck a golf-ball between the tee and the green.

Persons of unblemished reputation and scrupulous integrity will entirely forget whether they took three or four strokes to get out of a bunker; the fact that their first drive went out of bounds, and that they were forced to play a second shot from the tee, escapes their memory in a way that non-golfers might deem incredible. It therefore often becomes a task of uncommon delicacy to remind an adversary of strokes that have apparently made no impression upon his memory, without seeming to cast aspersions upon his honesty of purpose. And when, on the other hand, he adduces conclusive evidence to prove that one has taken eight shots to reach the hole, after one has confidently declared oneself to be "dead" in five, it is difficult not to temper one's apologies with resentment.

The art of winning or losing at any game is never a very easy one to acquire, and at golf it is only a whit less objectionable to evince signs of unconcealed elation at being "five up" than it is to stride along with a pale face and set jaw, declining to utter a civil word in reply to one's opponent's sympathetic comments, just because one happens to be "five down".

My cousin, Colonel Waters, was one of those players with whom it was impossible to play unless he chanced to be winning. The look of concentrated loathing which he cast upon a more fortunate rival was enough to spoil the pleasure of any game, and as soon as he became "two down" he would adopt an attitude of mute melancholia that rendered him the least desirable golfing companion in the world. At Hoylake, indeed, Colonel Waters was very generally known as "Siloam" – he had, they flippantly said, such a troubled face!

In one respect it is fair to say that golf is a selfish pastime; it is perhaps the only game that a man can pleasurably and profitably play *all by himself*.

An attempt to play lawn-tennis all alone is seldom satisfactory; indeed, my uncle, Horace Biffin, is one of the few men I ever heard of who seems to have derived any amusement from this form of entertainment. Even so the result was often more interesting for spectators than for the single player. You see, Uncle Horace was compelled by the exigencies of the situation to lob his service very high into the air, in order that he might be able to run round to the other side of the net in time to return the ball; and he never dared to send it back with any violence if he wished to sprint round again in time to take his return. At the back of his mind, therefore, there lay the perpetual consciousness that he could always defeat himself if he desired, and this deprived the game of much of its interest, and robbed the player of a good deal of his natural zest. Uncle Horace, indeed, would often become so tired of rushing wildly round to the opposite court to take his own service that he was tempted now and again to serve eight consecutive faults into the net, so as to bring the set to an end; and it is not be wondered at that long before he had reached the age of eighty, he should have decided to renounce lawn-tennis in favour of golf.

At the latter game, as I have already remarked, a solitary player can enjoy a sufficiently exciting game either by matching himself with Bogey or by playing two balls, one against the other, from the tee. Colonel Waters, to whose eccentricities of conduct I have alluded above, when he began to find it increasingly difficult to persuade anybody to play with him, adopted the latter system, to his own and everybody's extreme satisfaction.

He would start out in the morning with two caddies, two sets of clubs, and two balls – a "Silver King" and a "Colonel" – and engage in the most thrilling contests against himself, from which he invariably emerged victorious. In these games he had no chance of displaying those peculiarities of temper which rendered him so unpopular among his fellows, for his rage at being laid a stymie by himself was mitigated by his feelings of joy at having laid himself a stymie; and whenever his "Silver King" rolled into a bunker, he found comfort in the fact that his "Colonel" was lying safely on the "pretty" or vice versa. Furthermore, he was enabled to invest the game with a spice of inexpensive adventure by laying a small shade of odds against either ball, and at the end of the day he could extract a morbid pleasure from writing himself a cheque for the amount he had won and lost, and sending it to the bank upon which it was drawn, to be placed to the credit of his account. Would that all gambling transactions – as the dear Dowager Bishop of Monte Carlo once said to me – would that all gambling transactions could be conducted so innocently, with so inconsiderable a loss of treasure and of *amour-propre*!

V

Among advanced Socialists and other persons who entertain
exaggerated views upon the Dignity of Labour, the use of a caddy
to carry clubs and construct tees is regarded as a grave blemish
upon an otherwise harmless pursuit. With equal justice one might
resent the employment of a groundsman to roll the pitch after each
innings at cricket, or consider that the presence of a professional
marker detracted from the merits of billiards.

The first-class caddy is in no sense of the phrase a beast of
burden; for the time being he becomes the sympathetic confidant,
often the autocratic adviser, of a man who is probably his superior
socially, intellectually, and financially. Indeed, the friendly
intercourse between player and caddy paves the way for that better
feeling between class and class which in these latter democratic
days affords so hopeful a sign of social regeneration.

As I write these words I cannot help recalling a touching scene
that indelibly impressed itself upon my mental retina, and to a
great extent bears out the truth of my contention. It was on the
links at Lossiemouth, last summer, when one of the greatest living
British statesmen was anxiously inspecting his ball as it lay in the
rough about thirty yards to the right of the eleventh hole.
Uncertain as to which club to select for so important an approach
shot, he turned for counsel to his caddy, a small Scottish lad of
some ten summers. The pair formed one of the prettiest pictures
imaginable: on the one hand the grey-headed but perplexed
statesman, gravely urging the advisability of taking a mashie; on the
other the ragged, bare-footed tousle-headed urchin, insisting upon
the use of a niblick. From the serious expression upon the eminent
politician's face he might well have been consulting a Cabinet

colleague upon some question of vital importance to the Empire, and I watched with interest to see the upshot of their deliberations.

It was all in vain that the hard-headed Minister of State, the man in whose hands lay the destinies of a great people, pleaded for his mashie; the bare-footed urchin stubbornly shook his head, and with an imperious gesture thrust the niblick into his employer's hand. Shrugging his shoulders in that resigned fashion that the House of Commons knows so well, the statesman took the proffered club, and in another moment had laid his ball within six inches of the hole. Do you wonder, dear reader, that as I turned away from this moving scene, with a lump in my throat and the tears starting to my eyes, I should have felt that I had at last learnt something of the qualities that render constitutional party government possible – that I had discovered, perhaps, some inkling of what it is that makes us Britons great? Yes – or rather, no.

VI

There comes a day, alas! in the lives of all of us when, under the stress of advancing years, the field-sports in which we were wont to indulge lose much of their pristine charm. The ping-pong racket is relegated to the lumber-chest, the skates hang rusting in the pantry cupboard, the beribboned oar is sent with the discarded cricket-bat to swell the Vicar's jumble sale, the croquet-mallet languishes among the grandchildren's perambulators in the telephone-room.

But though the niblick becomes a burden and the desire to drive a long ball from the tee fails, the golfer need not give way to utter despair. Even in his dotage he may still hope to extract a not altogether exiguous pleasure from striking a captive ball into a net in the back-garden, and can find endless satisfaction in the task of converting the lawn-tennis court into a putting-green for "clock golf". And when at last he is no longer able to leave the house, he can amuse himself by laying out a miniature golf-links in his wife's drawing-room, and dodder round with a couple of clubs, seeking to establish a record for the course.

In "house-golf" (as it is called) the various articles of domestic furniture will usually supply all the hazards required, though these may be further supplemented, if necessary, by obstacles imported from outside. Thus, a hip-bath filled with the moss-fibre in which last year's bulbs were grown makes an excellent bunker; two waste-paper baskets piled upon a low book-case add to the difficulties of a mashie-shot from the sofa on to the hearth-rug, where an inverted saucer adequately fulfils the purpose of a hole.

In the drawing-rooms of most of the Stately Homes of England little courses of this kind have been planned by loving hands, and the aristocratic inmates are thus provided with a source of innocent occupation that the most selfish Socialist could scarcely grudge them.

It is true that old Lady Chorlesbury used to point with horror to the holes made by her husband's niblick in the best Wilton carpet, and found but little comfort in his solemn promise to replace the divots, she nevertheless realized that it would be cruel to deprive the old gentleman of such a means of solace in his declining years, and at Chorlesbury House "drawing-room golf" was always winked at, if not actively encouraged.

I happened to be having tea there one evening last winter when Lord Chorlesbury tottered in on the arm of his valet and challenged me to a friendly game. To humour him I consented to play, though I had no nails in my boots, and was forced to borrow the butler's clubs.

On his own home links, I need hardly say, I was no match for my host, his knowledge of the course giving him a decided advantage, as was soon only too apparent. At the very first hole – a dog-leg round a lacquer screen, with a china cupboard guarding the green – after being stymied by a bust of the late Dr Livingstone and having on two occasions to lift my ball without penalty from casual ink on the writing-table I lost my nerve. And when, at the second I found myself in a hopeless lie behind a marble clock on the mantlepiece, I picked up in despair. I shall never forget his lordship's delight, later on in the game, on his becoming "Dormy Two", when a pretty approach shot of mine was caught by the keyboard of the piano, and I hooked my next into the coal-scuttle (taking three to get out), while with a fine lofting shot over an occasional table my host laid his ball dead on the hearth-rug in four.

Lady Chorlesbury watched the game with interest from a chair near the window, and it was tacitly agreed (in accordance with a local by-law) that whenever a ball struck her on the head and bounced off into the rough, the player should be allowed to have the strike over again; while if it remained in her lap, she should be regarded as "ground under repair", and the ball be lifted without a penalty.

Lord Chorlesbury was indeed a true sportsman; to the very end of his life he helped to keep alive that spirit of sport upon which our Imperial greatness so largely depends. One of his last acts was to despatch a postal order for five shillings to the Olympic Talent Fund when it seemed possible that the subscriptions might fall short by some £90,000 of the desired total. At his lamented demise, *Golf Illustrated* published a lifelike portrait of him, which I have cut out and hung in the spare bedroom; and when I am slicing badly, or have temporarily lost the art of "putting", I go and gaze at this picture of the man who provided the world with a perfect example of all that a Retired Golfer should be, whose handicap was never less than 30, but who never gave up hope. Peace to his mashies!'

## BEGINNER'S LUCK
A.G. MacDonell

'A few days after his curious experience on the cricket field, Donald's attention was drawn away from the problem of the Englishman's attitude towards his national game by a chance paragraph in a leading newspaper on the subject of Golf. And golf was a matter of grave temptation to Donald at this period of his life.

Both Sir Ethelred Ormerode, MP, and Sir Ludovic Phibbs, MP, had invited him to a day's golf at one or other of the larger clubs near London to which they belonged; but Donald had made

excuses to avoid acceptance, for the following reason. He had
played no golf since he had been a lad of eighteen at Aberdeen,
and as he had not enough money to join a club in the south and
play regularly, he was unwilling to resurrect an ancient passion
which he had no means of gratifying. Up to the age of eighteen
golf had been a religion to him far more inspiring and appealing
than the dry dogmatics of the various sections of the Presbyterian
Church which wrangled in those days so enthusiastically in the
North-East of Scotland. Since that time, of course, there has been
a notable reunion of the sections and public wrangling has perforce
come to an end, an end regretted so passionately that the phrase "a
peace-maker" in that part of the world is rapidly acquiring the
sense of a busy-body or spoil-sport. As one ancient soldier of the
Faith, whose enthusiasm for the Word was greater than his
knowledge of it, was recently heard to observe bitterly into the
depths of his patriarchal beard, "Isn't it enough for them to have
been promised the Kingdom of Heaven, without they must poke
their disjaskit nebs into Buchan and the Mearns?"

But whatever the rights and wrongs of the once indignant and
now cooing Churches, it is a fact that Donald before the war was
more interested in golf than in religion, and a handicap of plus one
when he was seventeen had marked him out as a coming man. But
first the War and then the work of farming the Mains of
Balspindie had put an end to all that, and Donald was reluctant to
awaken the dragon.

But one day he happened to read in one of the most famous
newspapers in the world the following paragraph in a column
written by "Our Golf Correspondent":

"Our recent defeat at the hands of the stern and wild Caledonians
was, no doubt, demnition horrid, as our old friend would have
said, and had it not been for the amazing series of flukes by which
the veteran Bernardo, now well advanced in decrepitude, managed
to hang on to the metaphorical coat-tails of his slashing young

adversary, but even to push his nose in front on the last green, the score of the Sassenachs would have been as blank as their faces. For their majestic leader was snodded on the fourteenth green, and even the Dumkins and Podder of the team, usually safe cards, met their Bannockburn. And that was that. The only consolation for this unexpected "rewersal" lies in the fact that the Northerners consisted almost entirely of what are called Anglo-Scots, domiciled in England and products of English golf. For there is no doubt that the balance of golfing power has shifted to the south, and England is now the real custodian of the ancient traditions of the game. Which, as a consolation prize, is all wery capital."

Donald read this through carefully several times, for it seemed to be a matter of importance to him and his work. He had seen, at very close quarters, the English engaged upon their ancient, indigenous national pastime, and he had been unable to make head or tail of it.

But it was worth while going out of his way to see how they treated another nation's national game which, according to the golf correspondent, they had mastered perfectly and had, as it were, adopted and nationalized.

The matter was easily arranged, and, on the following Sunday, he was picked up at the corner of Royal Avenue and King's Road by Sir Ludovic Phibbs in a Rolls-Royce limousine car. Sir Ludovic was wearing a superb fur coat and was wrapped in a superb fur rug. On the way down to Cedar Park, the venue of the day's golf, Sir Ludovic talked a good deal about the scandal of the dole. It appeared to be his view that everyone who took the dole ought to be shot in order to teach them not to slack. The solution of the whole trouble was the abolition of Trades Unionism and harder work all round, including Saturday afternoons and a half-day Sundays. This theme lasted most of the journey, and Donald was not called upon to contribute more than an occasional monosyllable.

Cedar Park is one of the newest of the great golf clubs which are ringed round the north, west and south of London in such profusion, and what is now the clubhouse had been in earlier centuries the mansion of a venerable line of marquesses. High taxation had completed the havoc in the venerable finances which had begun in the Georgian and Victorian generations by high gambling, and the entire estate was sold shortly after the War by the eleventh marquess to a man who had, during it, made an enormous fortune by a most ingenious dodge. For, alone with the late Lord Kitchener, he had realized in August and September of 1914 that the War was going to be a very long business, thus providing ample opportunities for very big business, and that before it was over it would require a British Army of millions and millions of soldiers. Having first of all taken the precaution of getting himself registered a man who was indispensable to the civil life of the nation during the great Armageddon, for at the outbreak of hostilities he was only thirty-one years of age, and, in order to be on the safe side, having himself certified by a medical man as suffering from short sight, varicose veins, a weak heart, and incipient lung trouble, he set himself upon the great task of cornering the world's supply of rum. By the middle of 1917 he had succeeded, and in 1920 he paid ninety-three thousand pounds for Cedar Park, and purchased in addition a house in Upper Brook Street, a hunting-box near Melton, a two-thousand-ton motor yacht, Lochtarig Castle, Inverness-shire, and the long leases of three luxurious flats in Mayfair in which to entertain, without his wife knowing, by day or night, his numerous lady friends. He was of course knighted for his public services during the War. It was not until 1925 that the rum-knight shot himself to avoid an absolutely certain fourteen years for fraudulent conversion, and Cedar Park was acquired by a syndicate of Armenian sportsmen for the purpose of converting it into a country club.

An enormous man in a pale-blue uniform tricked out with thick silver cords and studded with cartwheel silver buttons, opened the door of the car and bowed Sir Ludovic, and, a little less impressively, Donald Cameron into the clubhouse. Donald was painfully conscious that his grey flannel trousers bagged at the knee and that his old blue 1914 golfing-coat had a shine on one elbow and a hole at the other.

The moment he entered the clubhouse a superb spectacle met his dazzled gaze. It was not the parquet floor, on which his nail-studded shoes squeaked loudly, or the marble columns, or the voluptuous painting on the ceiling, or the gilt-framed mirrors on the walls, or the chandeliers of a thousand crystals, or even the palms in their gilt pots and synthetic earth, that knocked him all of a heap. It was the group of golfers that was standing in front of the huge fire-place. There were purple jumpers and green jumpers and yellow jumpers and tartan jumpers; there were the biggest, the baggiest, the brightest plus-fours that ever dulled the lustre of a peacock's tail; there were the rosiest of lips, the gayest of cheeks, and flimsiest of silk-stockings, and orangest of finger-nails and probably, if the truth were known, of toe-nails too; there were waves of an unbelievable permanence and lustre; there were jewels, on the men as well as the women, and foot-long jade and amber cigarette holders and foot-long cigars with glistening cummerbunds; and there was laughter and gaiety and much bending, courtier-like, from the waist, and much raising of girlish, kohl-fringed eyes, and a great chattering. Donald felt like a navvy, and when, in his agitation, he dropped his clubs with a resounding clash upon the floor and everyone stopped talking and looked at him, he wished he was dead. Another pale-blue-and-silver giant picked up the clubs, held them out at arm's length and examined them in disdainful astonishment – for after years of disuse they were very rusty – and said coldly, "Clubs go into the locker-room, sir," and Donald squeaked his way across the parquet after him amid a profound silence.

The locker-room was full of young gentlemen who were discarding their jumpers – which certainly competed with Mr

Shelley's idea of Life Staining the White Radiance of Eternity – in favour of brown leather jerkins fastened up the front with that singular arrangement which is called a zipper. Donald edged in furtively, hazily watched the flunkey lay the clubs down upon a bench, and then fled in panic through the nearest open door and found himself suddenly in a wire-netted enclosure which was packed with a dense throng of caddies. The caddies were just as surprised by his appearance in their midst as the elegant ladies and gentlemen in the lounge had been by the fall of the clubs, and a deathly stillness once again paralysed Donald.

He backed awkwardly out of the enclosure, bouncing off caddy after caddy like a cork coming over a rock-studded sluice, and was brought up short at last by what seemed to be a caddy rooted immovably to the ground. Two desperate backward lunges failed to dislodge the obstacle and Donald turned and found it was the wall of the professional's shop. The caddies, and worse still, an exquisitely beautiful young lady with a cupid's-bow mouth and practically no skirt on at all, who had just emerged from the shop, watched him with profound interest. Scarlet in the face, he rushed past the radiant beauty and hid himself in the darkest corner of the shop and pretended to be utterly absorbed in a driver which he picked out at random from the rack. Rather to his surprise, and greatly to his relief, no one molested him with up-to-date, go-getting salesmanship, and in a few minutes he had pulled himself together and was able to look round and face the world.

Suddenly he gave a start. Something queer was going on inside him. He sniffed the air once, and then again, and then the half-forgotten past came rushing to him across the wasted years. The shining rows of clubs, the boxes of balls, the scent of leather and rubber and gripwax and pitch, the club-makers filing away over the vices and polishing and varnishing and splicing and binding, the casual members waggling a club here and there, the professional listening courteously to tales of apocryphal feats, all the old familiar scenes of his youth came back to him. It was eleven years

since he had played a game of golf, thirteen years since he had bought a club. Thirteen wasted years. Dash it, thought Donald, damn it, blast it, I can't afford a new club – I don't want a new club, but I'm going to buy a new club. He spoke diffidently to one of the assistants who was passing behind him, and enquired the price of the drivers.

"It's a new lot just finished, sir" said the assistant, "and I'm not sure of the price. I'll ask Mr Glennie."

Mr Glennie was the professional himself. The great man, who was talking to a member, or rather was listening to a member's grievances against his luck, a ritual which occupies a large part of a professional's working day, happened to overhear the assistant, and he said over his shoulder in the broadest of broad Scottish accents, "They're fufty-twa shullin' and cheap at that."

Donald started back. Two pounds ten for a driver! Things had changed indeed since the days when the great Archie Simpson had sold him a brassy, brand-new, bright yellow, refulgent driver with a lovely whippy shaft, for five shillings and nine-pence.

His movement of Aberdonian horror brought him out of the dark corner into the sunlight which was streaming through the window, and it was the professional's turn to jump.

"It's Master Donald!" he exclaimed. "Yes mind me, Master Donald – Jim Glennie, assistant that was at Glenavie to Tommy Anderson that went to the States?"

"Glennie!" cried Donald, a subtle warm feeling suddenly invading his body, and he grasped the professional's huge red hand.

"Man!" cried the latter, "but I'm glad to see ye. How lang is't sin' we used to ding awa at each other roon' Glenavie. Man, it must be years and years. And fit's aye deein' wi' yer game? Are ye plus sax or seeven?"

"Glennie," said Donald sadly, "I haven't touched a club since those old days. This is the first time I've set foot in a professional's shop since you took me that time to see Alec Marling at Balgownie the day before the War broke out."

"Eh, man, but you're a champion lost," and the professional shook his head mournfully.

"But Glennie," went on Donald, "where did you learn that fine Buchan accent? You never used to talk like that. Is it since you came south that you've picked it up?"

The big professional looked a little shamefaced and drew Donald back into the dark corner.

"It's good for trade," he whispered in the pure English of Inverness. "They like a Scot to be real Scottish. They think it makes a man what they call 'a character'. God knows why, but there it is. So I just humour them by talking like a Guild Street carter who's having a bit of back-chat with an Aberdeen fish-wife. It makes the profits something extraordinary."

"Hi! Glennie, you old swindler," shouted a stoutish, red-faced man who was smoking a big cigar and wearing a spectroscopic suit of tweeds. "How much do you want to sting me for this putter?"

"Thirty-twa shullin' and saxpence, Sir Walter," replied Glennie over his shoulder, "but ye'll be wastin' yer siller, for neither that club nor any ither will bring ye doon below eighteen."

A delighted laugh from a group of men behind Sir Walter greeted this sally.

"You see," whispered Glennie, "he'll buy it and he'll tell his friends that I tried to dissuade him, and they'll all agree that I'm a rare old character, and they'll all come and buy too."

"But fifty-two shillings for a driver!" said Donald. "Do you mean to say they'll pay that?"

"Yes, of course they will. They'll pay anything so long as it's more than any other professional at any other club charges them. That's the whole secret. Those drivers aren't a new set at all. They're the same set as I was asking forty-eight shillings for last week-end, but I heard during the week from a friend who keeps an eye open for me, that young Jock Robbie over at Addingdale Manor had put his drivers and brassies up from forty-six shillings to fifty, the dirty young dog. Not that I blame him. It's a new form

of commercial competition, Master Donald, a sort of inverted price-cutting. Na, na, Muster Hennessy," he broke into his trade voice again, " ye dinna want ony new clubs. Ye're playin' brawly with yer auld yins. Still if ye want to try yon spoon, tak it oot and play a couple of roons wi' it, and if ye dinna like it put it back."

He turned to Donald again.

"That's a sure card down here. They always fall for it. They take the club and tell their friends that I've given it to them on trial because I'm not absolutely certain that it will suit their game, and they never bring it back. Not once. Did you say you wanted a driver, Master Donald?"

"Not at fifty-two shillings," said Donald with a smile.

Glennie indignantly waved away the suggestion.

"You shall have your pick of the shop at cost price," he said, and then, looking furtively round and lowering his voice until it was almost inaudible, he breathed in Donald's ear, "Fifteen and six."

Donald chose a beautiful driver, treading on air all the while and feeling eighteen years of age, and then Sir Ludovic Phibbs came into the shop.

"Ah! There you are, Cameron," he said genially; "there are only two couples in front of us now. Are you ready? Good morning, Glennie, you old shark. There's no use trying to swing the lead over Mr Cameron. He's an Aberdonian himself."

As Donald went, Glennie thrust a box of balls under his arm and whispered, "For old time's sake!"

On the first tee Sir Ludovic introduced him to the other two players who were going to make up the match. One was Mr Wollaston, a clean-shaven, intelligent, large, prosperous-looking man of about forty, and the other was Mr Gyles, a very dark man, with a toothbrush moustache and a most impressive silence. Both were stockbrokers.

"Now," said Sir Ludovic heartily, "I suggest that we play a four-ball foursome, Wollaston and I against you two, on handicap, taking our strokes from the course, five bob corners, half a crown for each birdie, a dollar an eagle, a bob best ball and a bob aggregate and a bob a putt. What about that?"

"Good!" said Mr Woolaston. Mr Gyles nodded, while Donald, who had not understood a single word except the phrase "four-ball foursome" – and that was incorrect – mumbled a feeble affirmative. The stakes sounded enormous, and the reference to birds of the air sounded mysterious, but he obviously could not raise any objections.

When it was his turn to drive at the first tee, he selected a spot for his tee and tapped it with the toe of his driver. Nothing happened. He looked at his elderly caddy and tapped the ground again. Again nothing happened.

"Want a peg, Cameron?" called out Sir Ludovic.

"Oh no, it's much too early," protested Donald, under the impression that he was being offered a drink. Everyone laughed ecstatically at this typically Scottish flash of wit, and the elderly caddy lurched forward with a loathsome little contrivance of blue and white celluloid which he offered to his employer. Donald shuddered. They'd be giving him a rubber tee with a tassel in a minute, or lending him a golf-bag with tripod legs. He teed his ball on a pinch of sand with a dexterous twist of his fingers and thumb amid an incredulous silence.

Donald played the round in a sort of daze. After a few holes of uncertainty, much of his old skill came back and he reeled off fairly good figures. He had a little difficulty with his elderly caddy at the beginning of the round, for, on asking that functionary to hand him "the iron" he received the reply, "Which number, sir?"

"Which number what?" faltered Donald.

"Which number iron?"

"Er – just the iron."

"But it must have a number, sir."

"Why must it?"

"All irons have numbers."

"But I've only one."

"Only a number one?"

"No. Only one."

"Only one what, sir?"

"One iron!" exclaimed Donald, feeling that this music-hall turn might go on for a long time and must already be holding up the entire course.

The elderly caddy at last appreciated the deplorable state of affairs. He looked grievously shocked and said in a reverent tone:

"Mr Fumbledon has eleven."

"Eleven what?" enquired the startled Donald.

"Eleven irons."

After this revelation of Mr Fumbledon's greatness, Donald took "the iron" and topped the ball hard along the ground. The caddy sighed deeply.

Throughout the game Donald never knew what the state of the match was, for the other three, who kept complicated tables upon the backs of envelopes, reckoned solely in cash. Thus, when Donald once timidly asked his partner how they stood, the taciturn Mr Gyles consulted his envelope and replied shortly, after a brief calculation, "You're up three dollars and a tanner."

Donald did not venture to ask again, and he knew nothing more about the match until they were ranged in front of the bar in the clubroom, when Sir Ludovic and Mr Wollaston put down the empty glasses which had, a moment ago, contained double pink gins, ordered a refill of the four glasses, and then handed over to the bewildered Donald the sum of one pound sixteen and six.

Lunch was an impressive affair. It was served in a large room, panelled in white and gold with a good deal of artificial marble scattered about the walls, by a staff of bewitching young ladies in black frocks, white aprons and caps, and black silk stockings. Bland wine-stewards drifted hither and thither, answering to Christian names and accepting orders and passing them on to subordinates. Corks popped, and the scent of the famous club fish-pie mingled itself with all the perfumes of Arabia and Mr Coty, smoke arose from rose-tipped cigarettes, and the rattle of knives and forks played an orchestral accompaniment to the sound of many voices, mostly silvery, like April rain, and full of girlish gaiety.

Sir Ludovic insisted on being host, and ordered Donald's half-pint of beer and double whiskies for himself and Mr Gyles. Mr Wollaston, pleading a diet and the strict orders of Carlsbad medicos, produced a bottle of Berncastler out of a small brown handbag, and polished it off in capital style.

The meal itself consisted of soup, the famous fish-pie, a fricassee of chicken, saddle of mutton or sirloin of roast beef, sweet, savoury, and cheese, topped off with four of the biggest glasses of hunting port Donald had ever seen. Conversation at lunch was almost entirely about the dole. The party then went back to the main club-room where Mr Wollaston firmly but humorously pushed Sir Ludovic into a very deep chair and insisted upon taking up the running with four coffees and four double kümmels. Then after a couple of rubbers of bridge, at which Donald managed to win a few shillings, they sallied out to play a second round. The golf was only indifferent in the afternoon. Sir Ludovic complained that, owing to the recrudescence of what he mysteriously called "the old trouble", he was finding it very difficult to focus on the ball clearly, and Mr Wollaston kept on over-swinging so violently that he fell over once and only just saved himself on several other occasions, and Mr Gyles developed a fit of socketing that soon became a menace to the course, causing, as it did, acute nervous shocks to a retired major-general whose sunlit nose only escaped by a miracle, and a bevy of beauty that was admiring, for some reason, the play of a well-known actor-manager.

So after eight holes the afternoon round was abandoned by common consent, and they walked back to the clubhouse for more bridge and much-needed refreshment. Donald was handed seventeen shillings as his inexplicable winnings over the eight holes. Later on, Sir Ludovic drove, or rather Sir Ludovic's chauffeur drove, Donald back to the corner of King's Road and Royal Avenue. On the way back, Sir Ludovic talked mainly about the dole.

Seated in front of the empty grate in his bed-sitting-room, Donald counted his winnings and reflected that golf had changed a great deal since he had last played it.'

# A HEAVENLY ROUND
Paul Gallico

'The funeral was mighty impressive. It was bound to be in the case of a man like Barnaby Jessup. Most of the town had turned out, and after it was all over, one of the pallbearers looked up at the sky and murmured "Be a nice afternoon for golf."

That remark might be considered to bear on the sacrilegious in view of the occasion, but none of the other pallbearers objected, and they were all old friends of Barnaby Jessup, men in their sixties or higher, all but one of them, and Barnaby Jessup had been seventy-six when they laid him to rest.

The six pallbearers walked back across the grave path to the car to take them back to town, and on the sidelines their names were spoken in hushed tones. For one of them, some years before, had been a candidate for president of the United States, one was a great surgeon in the land, a third, the youngest man of the lot, was a lean and tanned golf professional, winner of the Open, and it was he who had made the remark about golf.

The men got into the car and, as was natural, they talked about Barnaby Jessup on the ride back to town. But they did not reminisce about the time back in the 20s that Jessup had made a million in the stock market, nor about the way he had juggled railroads; it was of quite different matters that they talked.

The man who had almost become president said, "I was with Barnaby the day he put eight straight balls in the lake hole."

The surgeon, his eyes reflective, said thoughtfully, "I played with him the day he took a twenty-seven on a par three-hundred-and-ten-yard hole."

The mildest man of the group, the man who was simply the head of one of the late Jessup's holding companies, said, "I saw him wrap all of his clubs around a tree one afternoon," and no one commented, because that had been commonplace.

The car hummed across the black ribbon of road and there was a silence while the men privately considered their friend, and then finally the golf professional looked up at the warm blue sky and spoke quietly.

"I hope Barnaby finds a gold course," he said.


The gate before which Barnaby found himself was highly ornamental, of a curiously intricate wrought iron, and the pillars were of marble, but a marble which Jessup had never seen, marble with the lustre of a pearl.

"Ought to look into this," Jessup said. "The trustees could use it for the art museum."

And so saying, he passed through the gate and was presently

standing in the registrar's office where in due time he gave his name to a clerk, who wrote it down in gold letters.

"Glad to have you with us, Mr Jessup," the clerk said. "A good many of the inmates like to know why they've been able to come here. In your case – "

Jessup stopped him with a wave of his hand.

Like many men who have achieved great wealth and prominence, he was inclined to be autocratic. "I left an art museum behind," he said. "I divided my fortune among colleges and institutions – "

"Not for any of those things did you enter here," said the clerk.

Jessup was momentarily startled. "Well," he said, "I built the finest hospital in my state, equipped it with the best that money could buy, and brought some of the greatest medical men in the world – "

The clerk said, "That is entered on page three thousand one hundred and forty-nine under the heading Superficial Trivia."

Jessup was jarred right down to his heels by that one. He thought a minute and then began a recital of what he had done with his money, the charities he had supported, and before he had gotten under way with the list the clerk was shaking hs head negatively.

"You remember Jim Dolan?" said the clerk.

Jessup thought back down the years. "Jim Dolan," Jessup said slowly. "Must have been thirty years ago, that was. He was a caddie at the club. Killed in an accident."

"You went to see his mother," the clerk said, reading aloud from a page in the ledger.

"You had a meeting that was worth thousands to you, and you turned it down to go and see his mother."

"I didn't give her a dime," Jessup said. "Just called to pay my respects and tell her what a fine boy Jim had been. That's all I did."

"That's all," said the clerk gently, and smiled, and Barnaby Jessup scratched his head and wondered, but not for long, because he was a man of action and unaccustomed to being introspective.

"Look, son," he said, "all my life I've been on the go. I don't mean any offence, but tell me this, do I have to sit around on a cloud? I mean, just sit? And I've no ear for music, I can't play a harmonica, let alone a harp."

"Why, no," the clerk said. "You can do about anything you like; anything within reason, that is."

Barnaby hesitated and said in a low voice, "No golf courses in these parts, I suppose?"

"No country clubs," the clerk said. "There's no discrimination up here. But we have a very fine public course."

Barnaby Jessup smiled and then said, "I didn't bring my clubs. I – "

"Last door down on your left," the clerk said.

Barnaby had another question, but he kept it back because he didn't like to take too much of the clerk's time. And likely Pete Tyson wouldn't be up here anyway. Barnaby and Tyson had been business competitors and had fought each other with no rules and no holds barred, but most of all they had battled on the golf course. Ten years before, Barnaby had fought back the tears while he watched the clods go down over the mortal remains of his dearest enemy and closest friend.

He'd sure like to see old Pete. But a man can't have everything, he thought, and he went on down the hall to the last room on the left. A man sat at a bench inside and Barnaby stopped and stared, for he had never seen so many golf clubs. They lined the walls, clubs of every description.

"Help yourself," the man at the bench said without looking up.

Barnaby thanked him and selected a likely-looking driver from a case along one wall. It had the right feel with the weight in the head where he liked it. He tried the rest of the clubs and found them perfectly matched, and finally he put the set in a golf bag and half a dozen balls in his pocket.

"What do I owe you?" he said, taking out his wallet and extracting two one-hundred-dollar bills, for these were hand-designed bench clubs and he was ready to pay two hundred for all he had there, but not a penny more because he had always made it a practice not to let people take advantage of him because of his wealth.

"No charge," the man said, "They're your clubs. Look on the shaft."

Barnaby glanced down and saw his name stencilled there. "Well," he said in wonder, "but look here, I want to give you something, I don't doubt all employees up here are well treated, but just the same – "

The man squinted down the shaft of a club. "I'm no employee," he said. "I'm a permanent resident and a busy man."

Barnaby Jessup thanked him, walked to the door, then said, "Can you tell me how to reach the course?"

"Six miles due north."

"Is there a cab for hire?"

Barnaby couldn't understand what he said, it sounded like "Fly,"

and he didn't repeat the question, for the man was plainly
eccentric, athough a genius at his craft. He went outside to look for
a cruising taxi and then he felt something at his back when he slung
the golf bag over his shoulders and discovered that the strap was
tangled up with a protuberance growing out of his shoulders.

He wiggled his shoulder blades, and the next thing he knew he
was three feet off the ground and treading air, with both wings
flapping.

"Well, I'll be," Jessup said, then sighted on the sun, got a bearing
on what he considered to be due north, and took off, flying at a
steady, even clip about ten feet off the ground.

It was a trifle awkward; he got out of balance somehow while
trying to shift the golf bag and went into a tailspin and landed on
his chin in a gully, but it didn't hurt, and presently he was airborne
again, and then finally he saw a long stretch of green ahead of him
and he flew over the entire eighteen holes, surveying the layout.

When he had finished he knew he had just seen the ultimate in
golf courses. The fairways were gently undulating, lush with grass,
the greens like huge emeralds. It was a sporty course too, not too
flat, and yet not too hilly.

Getting quite excited, he flew back to the first tee, eager to swing
a club, for although he had been one of the world's most successful
men, it is said that no man achieves everything he wants in life and
Banaby Jessup had been a success at everything he turned his hand
to with the exception of golf. A not inconsiderable part of his
fortune had been spent on the game, but he had remained a duffer.
He had in his home a comprehensive library of golf from the
earliest works down to the most modern tomes. He had studied
under the greatest professionals in the world and had built in the
cellar of his home a cage where he would practice on such days
that inclement weather kept him off the course. But he had
remained a divot digger and a three putter down the years.

He made a neat two-point landing on the tee and as if by magic a
caddie bobbed up, a small freckled boy with a missing front tooth

who relieved him of his bag and handed him his driver.

"Howdy, Mr Jessup," the boy said. "Nice day for it."

Jessup stared at him. "Jim Dolan," he said. He couldn't see any mark on the boy from the truck. "Well, Jim," he said, "Like old days."

"Smack 'er out there, Mr Jessup," the boy said.

Jessup stood at the tee, addressing the ball and sighting towards the green, four hundred yards distant. Then he ran through the rules, cautioning himself not to press, to keep his head down, to start the club back low to the ground, to let the left arm do the work, to cock his wrists, and to shift his weight to the right foot with most of the weight on the heel.

He thought of all these things and then struck the ball, wincing a little as he always did, expecting either a hook or a slice. But he heard a musical little click, and the ball bounced on the fairway about two hundred and sixty yards away.

"Good shot," Jim said.

"Best one I ever hit," Jessup cried. "By juniper, I had it that time. I think I've figured this game out."

They walked forward to the ball and Jessup selected a brassie, sure that he was going to miss because never in his life had he put together two consecutive good shots.

He swung the brassie and that click sounded again and Jessup rubbed his eyes and said in awed tones, "It's on the green."

The caddie was already walking forward, handing Jessup his putter.

"I never made a par in my life," Jessup said. "I have a chance for a birdie. Oh, well I suppose I'll three-putt."

On the green he surveyed the situation, noticing the slope towards the pin. He jabbed at the ball, tightened up, but it rolled forward and fell into the cup.

Barnaby Jessup mopped his brow with a handkerchief and sat down on the apron at the edge of the green.

"Well," he said finally, "accidents will happen. Let's go, Jim. But maybe, at that, I will break one hundred today."

The second was a water hole. The lake sparkled a bright sapphire in the sun and the distance across the water was a hundred and eighty yards.

Jessup selected a spoon. "I should have brought more than six balls," he said. "Don't know why I didn't. I lose at least six every time I play. I'll put at least three in the lake."

He swung, then listened for the whoosh as the water received his offering, but he failed to hear it and neither did he see drops of water splashing upward.

"Lost sight of it," Jessup said.

"Good shot," the caddie said. "It's in the cup. It's a hole in one, Mr Jessup."

"Now wait a minute, Jim," Jessup said. "You're not supposed to lie up here. Besides, I'm an old man – "

"It's in the cup," the boy repeated.

Jessup was looking for a path around the lake when the boy took off and flew across and Jessup sailed after him. They landed on the green and sure enough the ball was in the cup.

He was too shocked to say anything, but assumed that every once in a while this kind of thing happened to everybody, a superlatively good day, but of course he'd go blooie any minute; he always had, he always would.

The next hole was three hundred and eighty yards and his drive was straight and far. They came up to it and the caddie handed him a seven iron.

"I usually use a five this far away," Jessup said.

"You can make it with the seven," Jim said.

Jessup didn't think so, but although he invariably took the hide off people who tried to advise him at business, he'd never somehow been able to disregard a caddie's advice.

Meekly he took the seven and swung. The ball landed on the edge of the green, bounced twice, rolled forward and fell into the cup. Jessup removed his glasses, blew on them and put them back on.

"You're playing a nice steady game," the caddie said. "Even two's at this point."

"I am not," Jessup said. "Don't be ridiculous, Jim. I can't possibly have played three holes and only taken six shots. Nobody could, no golfer in the world."

He took the scorecard from the boy and counted it, and counted it again on his fingers, and the boy was right, there was no disputing it. He had a three and a one and a two.

There was no getting away from it. It wasn't possible, but there it was. He was even two's.

He had started out with the eternal hope of breaking one hundred. Now he was afraid to think about it. But still, he told himself, he'd go blooie any moment now.

And when they stood on the fourth tee he was sure of it. Despite the fact that he was in Heaven, this hole might have been designed by the devil himself.

The fairway was perhaps forty yards wide with a dog leg in the distance. On the left was a gorge, the fairway ended abruptly, and beyond it was a vast nothingness; he could see clouds below it. A hooked ball was a goner.

"What happens to the ball if you hook it over the gorge?" Jessup said.

The boy's face was serious. "It goes all the way down," he said. "All the way."

"To the earth?" Jessup said.

And Jim Dolan shook his head. "All the way down."

Jessup took a second look and the clouds parted and he got a faint whiff of brimstone and saw a red glow burning madly for a moment.

"The only golf balls they get are the ones hooked over that gorge," the caddie said. "Poor devils."

Jessup placed his ball on the tee. On the right were the densest woods he had ever seen, and the fairway itself was sprinkled with traps. He took careful aim at a grassy spot between two traps and swung. He was afraid to look, and automatically he was reaching in his hip pocket for a second ball when the caddie said, "Nice shot."

And there was the ball, dead in the middle of the fairway.

They walked towards it and Jessup was shaking as though he had the ague, although it was as nice a day as a golfer could find, no breeze and not too hot, just warm enough to make a man's muscles feel loose.

They had almost reached the ball when they heard a sound in the woods to the right and a moment later a handful of dirt and pebbles came down out of the sky and then a ball dropped out of nowhere and landed in front of them.

Barnaby stopped and looked at a lean lanky figure coming out of the woods. He had a turned-down mouth and a bald and wrinkled pate and he was talking to himself. "By Saturn," he said. "By Venus, that was a shot."

Barnaby stared in amazement and then finally he found his tongue. "Pete Tyson, you old horsethief," he said.

"Well," Tyson cackled, "I never expected to see you here. What did you do, bribe the authorities?"

They shook hands and grinned at each other and then Tyson addressed his ball and he hadn't changed at all, Barnaby saw. Tyson wound himself into a pretzel until he was next door to strangling himself, then the club came down and the ball hopped across the fairway and disappeared over the edge of the gorge and down towards the licking red flames.

But his old partner had become philosophical, Barnaby had to admit that. "If it weren't for me," Tyson muttered, "they'd have a hell of a time down there." And he took another ball from his hip pocket, placed it on the turf and hit it towards the pin.

It was like old times playing with Pete Tyson, and Barnaby was so puffed up he could hardly wait to hit his ball. He could hardly contain himself, waiting to see the look on Tyson's face when he showed him how he was hitting the ball now.

Jim Dolan handed him a brassie and Barnaby stepped up and

swung, and when he raised his head the ball was lying on the green. He turned and looked at his friend and waited for him to say something.

But Tyson hadn't even opened his mouth. He just grunted and moved on down the fairway, and Barnaby stared at him, his face getting red.

They went along to the green and Barnaby sank a forty-foot putt and he looked up, and still Tyson hadn't said a word, and that was the last straw.

They went towards the next tee and Barnaby exploded. "Why don't you be a man?" he said. "I always knew I was the better golfer and now I've proved it. Why can't you be man enough to admit it? Just standing there and sulking like the cantankerous old goat you are."

"Hit the ball," Tyson growled. "If there's anything I hate it's a gabby golfer. You always did talk too much."

His face purple now, Barnaby stepped up without another word and hit the longest drive ever seen in the solar system. The ball went practically out of sight, then came down on the green and Jim Dolan handed him the putter.

And still Tyson's expression hadn't changed. Barnaby stood there, choking, while Peter hit his usual hundred-yard drive into the rough. They plodded along and Barnaby couldn't figure how Tyson had gotten up here, but it was obviously a mistake, and somebody had slipped up somewhere; some mix-up in the celestial filing system probably explained it. And instead of being grateful, Tyson was more ornery than he'd ever been down below, which was saying a good deal. And maybe Tyson wouldn't admit it, but anyway, Barnaby was going to beat the tar out of him.

And he did. They finished the first nine and Barnaby totted up his score.

Pete Tyson said, "Give me a sixty-three. Couple of bad holes, but I'll do better on the back nine. Let's have an ambrosia before we start out."

They walked up to the terrace and a waiter flew out with two tall and misty glasses.

Barnaby put his score card down on the table. "I have twenty-three," he said defiantly. "The caddie will vouch for it. I'll shoot about a forty-five for the eighteen."

He shoved the card under Tyson's nose, but the old goat just yawned and said nothing.

Barnaby sat there and told himself that he was the champion golfer of the universe. But somehow it left him cold, and suddenly he felt old and tired and even the ambrosia tasted flat. He sighed, put down his half-empty glass and got up slowly from the table.

"In a hurry?" Tyson grunted.

Barnaby said sadly, "Sorry Pete, but somehow I don't feel so good. I'm going to turn in my clubs. Don't think I'll play any more golf." And he thought that even if Tyson had congratulated him, he still wouldn't want to play any more.

Pete's wise old eyes squinted up at him and he chuckled dryly.

"Barnaby, you old fool," he said. "I shot a forty-six myself the first round I played here. It's one of the house rules."

"House rules?" Barnaby said, bewildered.

"They let you have up here what you don't get below," Tyson said. "You always wanted to be a perfect golfer. So did I. But somehow, most of the residents prefer to go back to being themselves. You can make your choice."

Barnaby didn't have to think twice for the answer to that one. And suddenly the sun came out and his loneliness was gone and he was itching to get out on the tee again.

"Tell you what," Tyson said. "On the back nine I'll play you for the ambrosia at the nineteenth. I'll give you three strokes."

"You'll give me strokes!" Barnaby's face was purple again.

"You've gotten hogfat since I saw you," Tyson said. "And besides, I've had lessons from Macpherson."

"Sandy Macpherson is up here?" Barnaby said in a whisper, for his was a name to conjure with.

"And where else would he be?" said Tyson. "So it's only fair I give you strokes. I wouldn't take advantage of you."

Barnaby's jowls shook with his laughter. "You'll give me strokes! Do I look like a man that takes candy from a baby! I never saw the day when I had to take strokes from a string bean of a man put together with baling wire. Strokes! Come on," he said. "I'm playing you even."

"Man, you'll rue the day," said Tyson, and their scowls wavered for a minute and became broad grins as the love they had for each other came through.

The caddies came up and they hurried across to the tenth tee. "Start it off," Barnaby said. "Give me something to shoot at if you can."

Tyson wound up and he missed the ball on his first try and swung again and got himself bunkered behind the ladies' tee.

"If I couldn't do better than that," Barnaby chuckled, "I'd quit."

He took his stance and then saw a stranger watching him, a hawk of a man with a blade for a nose, a man with sandy red hair and shrewd grey eyes, and a pipe in his mouth and a contemptuous dour look on his face.

"Meet Sandy Macpherson, our pro," Tyson said.

"Too bad we didn't meet earlier," Barnaby said. "I'd have liked a lesson from you, but I'll not be needing one now, for I've finally grooved my swing."

"Then swing, laddie, and dinna talk sae much," said Macpherson.

Barnaby waggled his club over the ball and ran over the rules in his mind and started back with the left hand and kept his eye on the ball and pivoted with the hips and shoulders and did everything according to the book – or so he thought. But there was a whooshing sound like a wet sock falling on a concrete floor and the ball blooped into the air and came down in a meadow to the right of the fairway.

"You'll have to hit another," Tyson cackled. "The Elysian fields are out of bounds."

Hit another he did, a topped dribbling shot, and he turned to Sandy Macpherson.

"I'd better have a lesson tomorrow," Barnaby said. "I must have done something wrong."

"Something!" said Macpherson with a laugh like a rusty safe door opening. "Ye dinna keep yere head doon."

"No, sir," said Barnaby, humble and ashamed.

"Ye swing like an old witch wi' a broomstick."

"I suppose I do," Barnaby said meekly, bowing his head for shame.

"Hoot," said Macpherson, "I'll hae to throw yere game away, mon. I'll hae to start from scratch and see if there's aught to be done wi' ye. Ten o'clock sharp tomorrow."

"Yes, sir," said Barnaby. "I'll be there." He grinned at Tyson, who was grinning back at him, and they started out to hunt for his ball in the Elysian fields, whistling a tune of his youth, and happy as a lark.'

# ACKNOWLEDGEMENTS

The compiler and publishers are grateful to the following for permission to reprint material that is in copyright:

Peter Alliss – from *The Duke* by Peter Alliss

Julian Barnes – from *The History of the World in 10½ Chapters* by Julian Barnes, reproduced by permission of Peters Fraser & Dunlop Group Ltd

John Betjeman – from 'A Subaltern's Love Song' by John Betjeman, in *The Collected Poems of John Betjeman* (Murray, 1958; expanded, 1962), by permission of John Murray (Publishers) Ltd

John Buchan – from *The Thirty-Nine Steps* by John Buchan (1915), by permission of A. P. Watt Ltd on behalf of The Lord Tweedsmuir and Jean, Lady Tweedsmuir

Agatha Christie – from *The Murder on the Links* by Agatha Christie, by permission of Agatha Christie Ltd

F. Scott Fitzgerald – from *The Great Gatsby* by F. Scott Fitzgerald (1925). Reprinted with permission of Scribner, a Division of Simon & Schuster, from *The Great Gatsby* (Authorized Text) by F. Scott Fitzgerald. Copyright 1925 by Charles Scribner's Sons. Copyright renewed 1953 by Frances Scott Fitzgerald Lanahan. Copyright © 1991, 1992 by Eleanor Lanahan, Matthew J. Brucoli and Samuel J. Lanahan as Trustees under Agreement Dated July 3, 1975 Created by Frances Scott Fitzgerald Smith

Ian Fleming – from *Goldfinger* by Ian Fleming © Glidrose Productions Ltd, 1959. Reproduced with the permission of Ian Fleming (Glidrose) Productions Ltd

Paul Gallico – 'A Heavenly Round' by Paul Gallico, copyright 1936, 1937, 1938, 1939, 1941, 1942, by Paul Gallico, used by permission of Gillon Aitken Associates

Harry Graham – 'I Was Playing Golf the Day the Germans Landed', from *More Ruthless Rhymes for Heartless Homes* by Harry Graham(1930); 'Retired Golf' by Harry Graham, both by permission of Laura Dance for the Estate of Harry Graham

Michael Green – from *The Art of Coarse Golf* by Michael Green (Robson Books, paperback edition, 1995)